The Management Guide to
Internet
Resources, 1997 edition

An Internet Primer and Guide
to Organizational Behavior,
Human Resource Management,
Operations Management,
and Strategic Management Resources

McGraw-Hill Series in Management

Consulting Editor
Fred Luthans

Titles of related interest selected from the McGraw-Hill Series in Management:

The Management Guide to
Internet
Resources, 1997 edition

An Internet Primer and Guide
to Organizational Behavior,
Human Resource Management,
Operations Management,
and Strategic Management Resources

BYRON J. FINCH

Miami University
Oxford, Ohio

The McGraw-Hill Companies, Inc.

New York St. Louis San Francisco Auckland Bogotá Caracas Lisbon
London Madrid Mexico City Milan Montreal New Delhi
San Juan Singapore Sydney Tokyo Toronto

McGraw-Hill

A Division of The McGraw·Hill Companies

The editors were Adam Knepper and Joseph F. Murphy;
the production supervisor was Kathryn Porzio.
The cover was designed by Christopher Brady.
R. R. Donnelly & Sons Company was printer and binder.

The Management Guide to Internet Resources, 1997 Edition

1 2 3 4 5 6 7 8 9 0 DOC DOC 9 0 9 8 7 6

ISBN 0-07-021718-1

Library of Congress Catalog Card Number: 96-77000

Contents

About the Author

Byron J. Finch received his B.S. and M.S. degrees from Iowa State University and a doctorate in operations management from the Terry College of Business Administration at the University of Georgia. He is professor of Management in the Richard T. Farmer School of Business Administration at Miami University in Oxford, Ohio, where he teaches undergraduate and graduate courses in operations management. Dr. Finch has co-authored several books, including *Spreadsheet Applications for Production Operations Management* (Richard D. Irwin) and *Operations Management: Competing in a Changing Environment* (Duxbury Press). He has been involved in production planning and quality management consulting projects in the food processing and paper processing industries. His research interests range from production planning and control and spreadsheet applications to using the Internet to improve product quality. Dr. Finch has published in such journals as *Academy of Management Journal, Journal of Operations Management, International Journal of Production Research, Production and Inventory Management Journal, International Journal of Quality and Reliability Management, Journal of Education for Business, Journal of Management Education,* and *LOTUS* .

Preface

To the Student:
The Internet can provide you with a wealth of information or a nightmare of frustration, depending on your perspective and on your ability to use it efficiently. By taking advantage of the references and descriptions presented in *The Management Guide to Internet Resources*, you will be able to exploit the Internet for all of its potential, at a minimal cost of time for you. While learning to add to your resources by tapping into the Internet's millions of pages, you will also begin to use the Internet for information other than that needed for your coursework. It will become a natural reaction for you to seek out information of all types on the Internet, opening up an alternative which will contribute substantially to your life-long learning endeavors.

To the Instructor:
The Management Guide to Internet Resources is designed to enhance any management class, from introductory undergraduate to advanced graduate levels, including those devoted to organizational behavior, human resource management, operations management, strategic management, business ethics, entrepreneurship, and more. It provides resources which range from the very specific to the very general and, through the very nature of the resources themselves, reinforces the true integrative nature of business. The information provided can save students and instructors many hours of searching the Internet for that one perfect site, minimizing wasted time and frustration on the part of the student and helping the instructor move the class to the point of using the Internet efficiency, productively, and painlessly.

Acknowledgments

I wish to express my appreciation to students, staff, and faculty of the Richard T. Farmer School of Business Administration at Miami University (Ohio) for their support on this project. I also thank my editor, Adam Knepper, at McGraw-Hill, for his support and ideas, his willingness to take a risk on this project, and for providing some Web sites.

Chapter 1

An Introduction to the Internet

About this Book

The first three chapters of this book are designed to give you a little information about the Internet up front, on a "need-to-know" basis only, just to get you started. The remainder of the book provides extensive resources that are useful for all management students and professionals. These resources are particularly useful for those who are interested in human resource management, operations management, organizational behavior, and various aspects of strategic management, including business strategy, business ethics, international management, and entrepreneurship. An appendix is also provided to supply information on several broad-based business resources outside of management, including some in finance and marketing.

This book is **not** intended to be a technical manual on the inner-workings of the Internet. It was intentionally written from a perspective that is not technical at all. Instead, it has been written from a user's perspective. In other words, the organization, structure, and mechanics of the Internet are addressed from the perspective of *how you can use them, how you most likely will use them, and what they offer,* not how they work.

In order for you to effectively use this resource, it is assumed that you have a minimal level of experience with personal computers. Whether you are a Windows or Mac user, if you can find your way around your word processor, you know enough to become quite proficient at navigating the Internet. It is also assumed that you have Internet access, either through a university, your company, or through an Internet service provider (ISP).

This book will enhance your ability to **efficiently** access and use resources available on the Internet. It includes only that information you *need* to know in order to accomplish one overriding objective:

Exploit the Internet:
Get the most from it, with the least possible cost

That cost is not dollars--it is more likely to be time and frustration. Right now, both are probably more important to you than dollars. Once you reach a level of expertise, however, wasted time and unnecessary frustration won't be a concern. You'll find that with experience and help, you can virtually eliminate the wasted time and needless frustration that is sometimes associated with using the Internet. This book is designed to guide you during that transition. Eventually, you will reach a point where you don't need a book to help you find things on the Internet. You'll use the Internet for that. Unfortunately for new users, the Internet can drain many hours from your allotment of time. As a student or a professional, you don't have time to waste, nor can you afford the frustration that can accompany learning to exploit this resource.

The Internet Defined

Put very simply, the Internet is a global collection of independently operating, but interconnected, computers. This massive collection of computers is quite diverse, containing everything from supercomputers to the large mainframes of government, business, and universities, to the small PC's in individuals' homes. It's more than a computer network, its a *network of computer networks*. While the existence of this network of interconnected computers creates a powerful entity, the real *value* to us is in the information it makes available. Each of the nodes of this world-wide network can independently store massive amounts of information. That's a lot of power, but it doesn't give us access to the information they hold. For us, the phenomenal value and power of the Internet is rooted in the fact that these computers are linked together. They can talk to each other, they can allow *us* to talk to each other, **and** they can access, read, and retrieve each other's information. In fact, anyone with access to a computer that is part of this huge network can access information in any other computer *if* that information is stored in such a way as to make it accessible to the public. This has resulted in a phenomenon that has progressed far beyond what most of us would have predicted a decade ago, and is certain, within a few years, to advance beyond what any of us can now imagine.

Fortunately for us, there is a tremendous amount of information that has been stored in just the right way--so we can access it, explore it, and even download it if we want to. In essence, being able to link to one of the computers in the network gives us access to all of the information on the entire network. In addition to being able to access information stored on these computers, anyone with Internet access can communicate with anyone else having access. The result is the ability to access immense amounts of information and communicate easily with people around the globe. The ability to sit at a PC at home or in a computer lab, and retrieve information stored in any of thousands of computers distributed around the world or to "chat" with someone thousands of miles away, yields a tremendous source of power. It means that hundreds of resources directly related to the various aspects of management can be explored. Access to information gives us the opportunity to learn more. Learning more gives us greater skills and greater knowledge. Skills and knowledge give us advantage. As managers, we want every advantage available.

Anyone who pays attention to the written and broadcast media has probably heard various accounts of the rapid rate of growth of Internet. This rapid rate of growth means that the Internet is becoming a normal and expected medium for communicating. It is no longer the exclusive domain of "computer geeks" and "techno-weenies." It has become an expected part of the set of tools any manager must have. To some extent this places an added burden on you, because you will be expected to be familiar with the Internet and proficient at using it by virtually any progressive organization you work for.

This rapid growth of the Internet means that the amount of information available on it is growing as well. On the upside, growth makes it more likely that what you are looking for is out there somewhere. The downside of this rapid growth, however, is that as the Internet grows, the speed at which information flows may slow down. Until major technological improvements to the Internet are made, it will become more difficult and time consuming for you to find what you are looking for.

A Brief History

A little historical perspective is useful for getting a better understanding of the Internet and its capabilities. The oldest relative of what we now call the Internet was ARPANET, created by the Advanced Research Projects Administration (ARPA) as a means of connecting three computers. It was completed in 1969. It quickly grew until it linked many military computers. The real elegance of the system was that it used a networking approach known as *dynamic routing*. Dynamic routing meant that there were many ways to link up to a desired computer and it would use whichever way was possible. With dynamic routing, if one route was ever destroyed or inoperable, the linkages and communication could still go on.

ARPANET was so popular that, as a result of adding linkages to universities, it became impossible to effectively manage. The unmanageable size resulted in ARPANET being split into two parts. MILNET consisted of strictly defense-oriented sites, while a new smaller ARPANET was dedicated to nonmilitary sites. The technical capability of ARPANET to communicate with MILNET was known as Internet Protocol (IP). IP was capable of far more than making it possible for two networks to communicate. With IP, it would be possible for thousands of networks to communicate.

By the early 1980's, with the move away from mainframe computing toward workstations, the potential number of computers linking to ARPANET suddenly became huge. It was enough to totally overwhelm the ARPANET.

The National Science Foundation (NSF) planned to fund several supercomputers that could be used by researchers throughout the U.S. via ARPANET. The plan to use ARPANET was never completed, but NSF did develop its own network, NSFNET. NSFNET connected a number of regional networks, which in turn connected all of the users in a region. There was such a mass migration from ARPANET to NSFNET that ARPANET was shut down in 1990.

While NSFNET was doing quite well, NSF's plan to fund access to supercomputers didn't come to fruition. NSFNET had developed a life of its own, however, and despite the fact that the supercomputers which NSFNET was designed to link didn't exist, NSFNET survived. By the mid-1990's many commercial Internet networks, all using the IP technology developed for ARPANET and MILNET, had taken on what NSFNET had started. There are now many IP providers, not just in the U.S., but throughout the world. These IP providers are the backbone of what we now call the Internet.

Internet Navigation: A Necessary Skill

Having access to such an awesome amount of information is of no value unless it is taken advantage of. The person who has access to valuable information, but chooses to ignore it, is no better off than the person who isn't even aware the information is out there. You might think that being able to navigate the 'Net would be a *nice*, but certainly not *necessary* skill. Wrong. The expectation that you add navigating the Internet to your inventory of skills is justifiable and desirable for several reasons. First, and most immediate, is that millions of informational resources become accessible to you. This has profound potential for the quality of work you do as a student of management and as a professional. The projects you are challenged with now, in all of your classes, can be enhanced substantially by your ability to access this huge repository of information.

Second, independent of *what* information you obtain from the Internet now, the *process* of finding it is generalizable to many aspects of your current and future life. The inevitable exploration will expose you to new and exciting facts and perspectives. Whether it is the information for a course project which you are looking for, or something related to a hobby, or a future job, or merely interesting "stuff" that you encounter along the way, the ability to navigate the Internet will add to your sources of information and will very quickly become a skill you can't imagine being without. The Internet and the ability to use it is a valuable tool that can give you a distinct advantage over others in the competitive world of business and make many of your activities more enjoyable.

You have probably heard it mentioned on many occasions that we have entered the "Information Age." To put the importance of being "Internet literate" during the Information Age in perspective, imagine yourself in the distant past, having just entered the "Bronze Age." What must it have been like for people in the Bronze Age who did not have access to any bronze or for those who had it but didn't know how to use it? Being a manager without a link to the "information" of the Information Age won't be as bad as throwing stones as the neighboring clan attacks with hammered bronze spears, but it won't be pleasant. Just as the key to success in the Bronze Age was having and taking advantage of access to bronze, the key to success in the Information Age will be to have access *and* the ability to use information. The Internet is, and will continue to be, a primary means of obtaining that information. You will have to learn to exploit it.

As the Bronze Age progressed, just being able to work bronze wasn't enough. Some were more skilled than others, and they prospered. Merely knowing how to access and navigate the Internet won't be enough either. Those who can truly exploit it will prosper from it the most. They will be able to use it most efficiently, understand what it offers and what it doesn't, and know where to look for what they need. They'll have a distinct advantage.

Lastly, but from a long-term perspective maybe most important of all, the Internet may provide one of the most important means for independent life-long learning. As the world in general, and the world of business, go through rapid change, the ability to keep up by reading books becomes more and more difficult. At the rapid rate of technological change, particularly in business, a book is obsolete the day it is printed. The speed at which all types of information can be made available through various electronic media makes the Internet an extremely attractive means of transferring information, especially if that information has a short life span or is constantly changing. The fact that you can access its information from home, work, or anywhere you can plug in a phone line makes this information extremely portable and readily available.

You may not like to think about it, but the next phase of your education will begin as soon as you finish this one. Another one will begin after that. The world is changing at such a rapid rate that your education will be obsolete within a few years. You will have to continue educating yourself to keep up with these changes. Information accessible through the Internet will enhance your ability to do that.

To put the chaos of the Internet into perspective, imagine yourself having a key to the door of a large library. Unfortunately, everyone else has a key also. Everyone has free access to put anything they want in the library, wherever they want to put it. To make matters worse, there is no librarian, there is no card catalog, no computerized index, no map, and no reference staff, so after people deposit materials, there is no structure to help others locate them. Despite the massive amounts of information, there is no logical organization or hierarchy to guide someone looking for something in particular. The Internet is like that library--a disorganized, chaotic repository of information. Some of the information is excellent and will be quite valuable to you. Some is of a general nature, while some is very narrow in application. Some of the information is merely useless, and some is pure garbage. We would probably not agree, however, on which is which.

Fortunately for those who don't have time to waste, tools have been developed to help locate things, even without any structure. With no standards, centralization, or authority, no single tool can be expected or depended upon to find everything. A comprehensive search for a particular topic can require the use of many different search tools and take many hours.

From this description, the Internet may not seem like the type of environment that would be of much value. With a basic understanding of the types of resources available, the tools that are most likely to help you find specific topics of interest, some guidance as to which ones might help most, and a large number of starting points for each management area, you will be able to enhance the work you do by exploiting Internet resources **efficiently,** with minimal effort and time. And you'll still have time to eat, sleep, and enjoy some spare time. You might be surprised to find, however, that you enjoy some of that spare time by surfing the Internet.

A Brief Disclaimer

There is one unavoidable weakness in any attempt to document Internet resources. No such listing can ever be completely current. The Internet is changing so fast, even references *about* the Internet located *on* the Internet are constantly out of date. While the reference portions of this book that describe the Internet, the types of resources contained, and how they can be accessed will remain current, some resources mentioned may remain current only as long as the individual or organization making them available chooses to do so. Because it is impossible to control access and accuracy of information at these sites, we can not take responsibility for their accessibility or accuracy. This book will, however, be updated frequently, and checked for accuracy as close as possible to press time.

Hopefully, by the time this book is obsolete, you won't need it anymore anyway. It will then be updated for your successor.

While you are mastering this new environment, however, we will keep you abreast of changes in addresses, new sites, and new tools. You can access that information through the McGraw-Hill College Division Homepage at:

http://www.mhcollege.com/

Updates and changes for users of this book can be accessed through the business section. Check it periodically for updates to the references identified in this book.

Chapter 2

A Functional Organization for the Internet

Types of Internet Resources

In many books written about the Internet, it's organization is presented as being a function of the technical means by which information is transferred or access is gained. For the typical user, this type of organization structure provides little value. If one's goal is to exploit the Internet for the knowledge it contains, it makes more sense to understand the organization of the Internet from the perspective of **what kind of information is there and how it might be used**. It is the information, after all, that we are after. From the perspective of their use, most of the resources you are likely to find helpful can be placed into two broad "functional" categories.

The first category could be described as containing "conversational resources," because that is precisely what they are. These resources allow you to take part in (or just eavesdrop on) conversations with individuals virtually anywhere. They lack the formality of other forms of publication on the Internet, but they are valuable just the same. There is nothing clandestine about the eavesdropping because everyone taking part knows that there are likely to be many more "lurkers" than active participants.

The second category will be referred to as "reference resources." These resources consist of text documents, graphics, videos, and sound files which can be accessed and downloaded. They are much more analogous to the books, periodicals, recordings, and videos available in a traditional library. The primary difference, however, is that they are much easier to publish electronically on the Internet than in hard copy, and much easier to access. From the standpoint of being able to transmit information easily and cheaply, the Internet has some great advantages. However, the ease of publishing on the Internet has removed any assurance of accuracy or real value of the resource. Anyone can electronically publish just about anything they want. This places a responsibility on you to filter the reliable from the unreliable.

The following sections provide some explanation about these two types of resources and a general discussion of how they are accessed.

Conversational Resources

Conversational resources are composed of two primary types: **mailing lists** and **newsgroups.**

Mailing Lists

Mailing lists are a very popular way to communicate with others on a particular topic. In essence, a mailing list, or "listserve," as it is often called, is a group of people who have decided to communicate by email and make everyone in the group privy to each message communicated between list members. Anyone interested can "subscribe" by having their name and electronic mail address placed on the list of members. All communication is sent to "the list" and everyone on the list receives a copy via email. Anyone who responds to a statement or query responds to the list, and everyone on the list is emailed the response. The computer that automatically distributes all communications is known as the "listserver" and merely acts as a reflector to send out all email communications to every list member. Subscription to the listserve is usually accomplished by sending a special email message to the listserver. Once subscribed, all messages come via email.

Listserves are usually created to enable members to focus on a particular subject. They tend to be quite narrow in scope. Listserve members are typically quite interested in and committed to the topic of the listserve because there is a substantial "cost" to being a member--large amounts of email. Some listserves are quite large, with hundreds of members, and can have very high levels of email traffic. People who subscribe and aren't very interested in the topic quickly become tired of the volume of email and remove themselves from the list. This often leaves a central group of "hardcore" members who carry on in-depth electronic conversations while others periodically join in or just observe.

Newsgroups

Newsgroups are similar to mailing lists in that they bring potentially large numbers of people with common interests together, but differ in how the access is obtained. The difference in access changes the personality of the group somewhat. A newsgroup is essentially an electronic bulletin board. Anyone can post an article to the board and it is read by anyone who chooses to read it. People can visit the board as frequently or infrequently as they want. Although queries and responses can take the same form as they do in a listserve, newsgroups often develop very different personalities from those of listserves. Because they do not require that someone subscribe to read them, newsgroups are often frequented by people who are less interested and not that committed to the particular topic on a long-term basis. They might have a fleeting interest or merely want to ask a question. Once answered, many are not likely to continue to read postings. There are usually some very committed readers on most newgroups, even as committed as members of listserves, but there will also be many who are "on the fringe." Since there is no cost, people are much more likely to come and go.

The larger number of casual and temporary group members results in lots of questions being posted that have been asked many times before. Most newsgroups address this problem by creating what is called a "frequently asked questions" (FAQ) list for people to review prior to posting a query. It is considered good form to read the FAQ list prior to posting to any newsgroup. The FAQ list is periodically posted as a newsgroup article (usually monthly) or it can be requested.

Because of their accessibility, newsgroups tend to have more of a transient population and may not form as much of a "virtual community" as often happens on a listserve. This may be part of the reason many newsgroups aren't very tolerant or patient with "newbies."

A query to either a listserve or a newsgroup will likely result in responses. Some will be friendly and helpful, some might not be so friendly and helpful.   Some might be inconsiderate or rude.   Such is life on the Internet. There will likely be experts in either place, but determining who is the expert and who isn't is not always easy.   Just as in any other conversation, the fact that individuals are active participants in virtual conversations doesn't mean they know what they are talking about. These individuals might or might not know more than you about the topic being discussed.   Likewise, the fact that someone chooses to "lurk" rather than actively take part doesn't mean they aren't knowledgeable, either.

Distinguishing between the knowledgeable and the ignorant is particularly difficult if you haven't observed the newsgroup or mailing list for very long.   The easiest way to learn who the knowledgeable people are is to monitor the newsgroup or list very closely and observe what goes on. Over time, those who don't contribute anything valuable will show their true colors.

Accessing Conversational Resources

Mailing lists can be joined if you have an email address.   They are relatively easy to subscribe and unsubscribe to.   You can subscribe and receive separate email messages for every message sent to the list or request a daily "digest" which will place all messages for the day into one email message.   This reduces the number of email messages, but can make it more difficult to quickly scan and sort all postings by their subject heading.

Many listserves also have an FAQ list which they will be happy to send to you. In many cases, the FAQ list is automatically sent when you subscribe.   The FAQ list is likely to answer many questions for you and reduce the likelihood that the same questions are answered repeatedly on the list. It will also provide you with a more accurate impression of what actually takes place on the listserve.   Many listserves also archive their messages and provide a site where you can perform keyword searches of past conversations.

Usenet newsgroups can be accessed by anyone with Internet access. Usenet can probably be accessed directly through your university's mainframe and can also be accessed through most Internet access providers.   There are over 14,000 Usenet newsgroups, on virtually any subject imaginable.   Your university might not access all of them, but you can probably request any that aren't available.   If you are accessing the

Internet through a university, an individual subscription to a newsgroup is usually not necessary. If you are accessing through an ISP, you may have to subscribe, but subscribing to a newsgroup is a very simple process. Usenet has been organized under a structured hierarchy. Table 1-1 provides the major headings and brief descriptions of the topics included in under each.

Table 2.1   Usenet Newsgroup Categories

Hierarchy	Topics Included
comp.	computer-related groups, usually very technical
sci.	science-related groups
rec.	newsgroups related to recreational activities
soc.	newsgroups related to social interests, cultures, religions, etc.
news.	newsgroups related to Usenet newsgroups
misc.	newsgroups that don't fit in any other categories
talk.	extensive arguments and debate
alt.	alternative groups, off the mainstream, no restrictions or formal process for getting a group included

A particular newsgroup can be accessed as frequently or infrequently as desired. There are also tools that will search archives of newsgroup articles for particular topics.

Reference Resources

The two types of reference-oriented resources you are most likely to find useful are **Gopher** and the **World Wide Web**. There are others that play a minor role, but these two will provide you with virtually anything you need.

Gopher

Gopher sites are often maintained by government agencies or by educational institutions. They contain text-only documents that can be accessed for viewing or for download through the Gopher system. The Gopher system lets you find information stored at these sites by using hierarchical menus. Prior to the development of browsers (to be discussed in the next section) Gopher was used by accessing the desired computer through a program known as *telnet*. Although it can still be accessed in that manner, it is probably much easier to access using a browser. Gopher sites contain such documents as regulations, policies, and reports of governmental agencies and research reports of educational institutions. The entire range of information accessible through Gopher, known as Gopherspace, covers a broad variety of topics.

The World Wide Web

The fastest growing sector of the Internet is that portion that utilizes hypertext markup language (HTML) to transfer text, sound, graphics, and video, known as the World Wide Web (WWW or the web).   As of December, 1995, its growth rate was estimated to be doubling in size every 53 days. This estimate has been claimed as being optimistic by some, but there is no question that the web is growing at a phenomenal rate.

The web differs from Gopher in that its documents, known as "pages" are full of graphics and color, include sound and video, and are written in *hypertext*. Hypertext is a form of text which allows the writer to link words in the text to other documents, graphic images, video, or even Web pages stored on the other side of the world. Hypertext empowers the reader to explore a document only as deeply as desired. For example, while reading a document about the use of teams to plan major projects, one might encounter the word "leadership."   If "leadership" was designated a *hyperlink,* the reader could put the cursor on the word, click the mouse, and instantly examine a document it was linked to. It might be a document on the characteristics of strong leaders, for example. Or the reader could skip over the hyperlink and continue reading. The existence of hyperlinks is one of the key attributes that separates the Web from the rest of the Internet.

The following figure provides a model of the portions of the Internet most likely to be accessed for management-related information

Figure 2.1 A Functional Model of the Internet

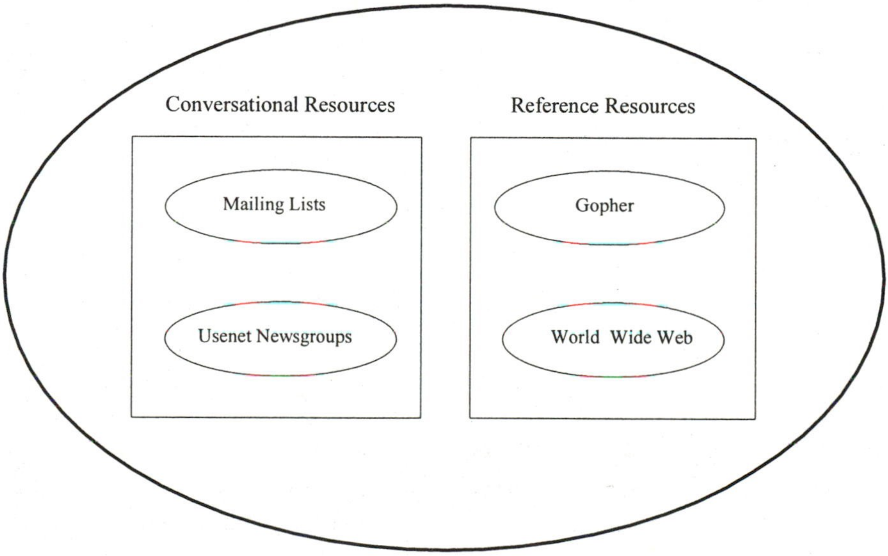

Conversational Resources   Reference Resources

Mailing Lists   Gopher

Usenet Newsgroups   World Wide Web

Accessing Reference-oriented Resources with a Browser

In the dark ages of the Internet (early 1993 and before) different programs were required to access different types of Internet resources. Then Marc Andreessen and Eric Bina, two students at the University of Illinois, developed *Mosaic*, a simple, graphical overlay, for the web. Mosaic was an instant hit. Shortly after Andreessen graduated and took a job with a firm in California, he was approached by Jim Clark, founder of Silicon Graphics, to start a new venture. With the combined talents of Clark,

Andreessen, Bina, and others, *Netscape* was born. Netscape's Navigator became available (for free) in April of 1994. It took over as the browser-of-choice immediately, claiming 70% of the browser market. Netscape is not the only browser, however. There are others in existence and there are sure to be more developed.

The browser lets us access all of the features of the web and access Gopher and Usenet as well. If you have Internet access, an email address, and access to a browser, you can access any of the resources listed in the remainder of this book. The browser has become a critical component of accessing the Internet. The following short section will provide enough basic information to help you get familiar enough with yours to make it work for you. Because of its popularity, when specificity is necessary, examples will be provided from the perspective of using Netscape. Most commands, however, are so similar from one browser to another, that they are very generalizable. The key differences between browsers comes not in *what* they do, but in *how* they do it. They vary in how fast they work, how pretty the resource looks when you finally see it, whether they can handle the latest enhancements to HTML, and other features. They will all take you where you want to go, however.

A Quick Guide to Using a Browser

The core of the browser's value is its ability to take an address from us and link to that particular file on that particular computer. The address used by the browser is known as a URL, for "Uniform Resource Locator." URL's always start with the *scheme* and then give specific information in the form of a path to a particular computer and a particular resource on that computer.

The scheme can be one of several, the most common being

      http://

which is the notation used to indicate that the resource being sought is a web page (the "http" stands for hypertext transfer protocol). Although "http://" is the most common scheme you will encounter, you'll also have use for several others:

      gopher://   Indicates a resource at a Gopher site.

mailto://   Brings up an email form pre-addressed to the
        email address specified in the URL.

As an example, let's take a look at a typical URL. The author's home page on the web is in a file called "index.html" on the "www" subdirectory of his account on Miami University's mainframe. A ".edu" in a URL indicates a location at an educational institution. A ".com" would indicate a business, and a ".gov" would indicate a government site. In the case of the author's URL, a nice convention of the browser is taken advantage of. Browsers automatically look for a file named "index" and go to it. Since the author's home page is named "index.html," there is no need to even mention it in the URL. If the browser is sent to his account, it will automatically go to index.html. The URL is as follows:

   http://www.muohio.edu/~bjfinch/

The author maintains another WWW page for students in his classes. This page is in a file, in the same subdirectory, and is named "ominfo.html." The URL for this page is:

   http://www.muohio.edu/~bjfinch/ominfo.html

A browser works like a map and compass. If you want to visit old friends and know exactly where they live (state, city, street, house number), the map and compass will help you get there. If you don't know where they live, however, the map and compass are of little use. You need to find out what their address is. Finding addresses of places you wish to visit is the biggest challenge, the biggest frustration, and the biggest consumer of time on the Internet.

If you are using the Netscape browser, to tell it where you wish to go, simply click on **open** and then type in the URL, hit **enter** or click on **open**, and you are on your way. Your browser also has several other important capabilities. It allows you to save documents you wish to take with you, print documents, or immediately return to your **home** page. The **forward** and **back** arrows allow you to quickly move back and forth between sites you've visited and the **reload** function allows you to reload a page that was not communicated correctly. The **bookmark** function, described in greater detail later, allows you to create a list of addresses you frequent. Your browser also has links to popular sites and some simple search tools.

Chapter 3

Finding What You Want

Search Engines

Searches for Internet resources can be performed in several ways. They are probably most effectively done by performing keyword searches on tools designed specifically for that purpose. Some search tools are specific to Usenet newsgroups, some work only in Gopher, others only on the web, and still others cross these boundaries. The search tools, known as "search engines" provide a list of results or "hits" that match the keywords entered. There is no "best" search tool. They all have strengths and weaknesses. Don't assume that you can perform an exhaustive search using one tool. You can't. A thorough search will require the use of several different engines.

Before You Start. . . .

Before you begin any search, there are several ways to improve your efficiency. Anyone who has done much research on the Internet has found an interesting site, only to forget where it was and never be able to find it again. This is most likely to happen on sites that aren't found directly through a search engine--those times when one site takes you to another and that one takes you to another, and after several stops you find yourself at the very place you were looking for. It can be very difficult to find such a site again. This is an extremely frustrating experience, but fortunately one that can be prevented with a little foresight.

The easiest way to prevent this from happening is by being familiar with the "bookmark" or "hotlist" feature of your browser. All browsers allow you to easily record the URL of a site of interest so you can return to it later. When you find a site of particular interest, click on **bookmark** and then **add**, and the site will be recorded in your bookmark list.

If you are using a computer that others have access to, such as one in a computer lab, you will not be able to create a bookmark list on that computer. You can solve that problem by creating a bookmark file for storage on a diskette to take with you and use at any other computer.

If the browser is Netscape version 1.n, the first time you use it, add any desirable sites to the bookmark list by using the **add** feature. When you are ready to stop using the browser, click on **bookmarks**, then **view bookmarks**. Select **edit** in the bottom corner of the bookmark list window. In the now-expanded bookmark list window, select **export bookmarks**. The default file name will be *bookmark.htm*. Select drive *a:*, if that is the location of your diskette. The bookmarks you've added will be exported to a *bookmark.htm* file on your diskette. The next time you use the browser, prior to doing any searching, go through the same process, but select **import bookmarks** instead of **export bookmarks**, and select *bookmark.htm* from your diskette as the source. This will bring all of your stored bookmarks into the browser's bookmark list. When finished, export the bookmarks back to your diskette again. If you work on different computers, even if one is your home computer, this technique allows you to bring your bookmarks with you wherever you go.

An alternative to importing and exporting bookmarks to a file on a diskette, if your browser is Netscape 1.n, is to click on **options,** then **preferences**. Select **applications and directories** from the list in the box at the top of the window. In the box next to **Bookmark File** type *a:\bookmark.htm* then click **OK**. Restart Netscape and it will look to the *a:\bookmark.htm* file for its bookmarks and store any that are added to that file.

If you are using Netscape version 2.0 or later, the process is a little different, but simpler. When you wish to add sites to the bookmark list, click on **bookmarks**, then **add**. Or, if you wish to add a bookmark directly from the hyperlink, without actually visiting the site, use the right mouse button and select **add bookmark for this link**. When you are ready to leave the computer and take the bookmark list with you, select **bookmarks**, then **go to bookmarks**. Then select **file**, then **save as** and enter the file name you wish to give your bookmarks. If you wish to save it to a diskette in the a: drive, be sure to prefix the filename with a:\. Also be sure to give it a .htm suffix.

As an even greater precaution, particularly after you have developed a valuable bookmark list, while in your browser, select **file** and then **open file** instead of **open location**. Type the path to your bookmark file, a:\bookmark.htm, for example, and you will be able to view it. Select **print** and you will receive a hard copy of your bookmark list.

It is sometimes convenient, while using your browser, to have a word processing program open at the same time. Working back and forth between the browser and word processor, using the ALT-TAB toggle in Windows, allows you to quickly block copy the URL of an interesting site or comment about its contents to a text document.

Searching Newsgroups

If you would like to monitor one Usenet newsgroup, or even several, and aren't sure which one meets your needs, a great place to start is with the newsgroup: **news.announce.newusers.** It contains an alphabetical listing of all newsgroups. If you are overwhelmed by the list of over 10,000, or are unable to find any that deal with the particular topic you are interested in, there are still ways to proceed.

One approach is to perform a keyword search of the FAQ lists of newsgroups. If the FAQ contains questions that are of the topic you're interested in, it not only provides an indication that this newsgroup might be a good choice, but you can also access the entire FAQ list. You may find answers to questions without having to go any further.

Infoseek Guide   http://guide.infoseek.com/

Infoseek Guide offers keyword searches of the FAQ lists so you can identify Usenet newsgroups that meet your needs. The results of a keyword search of FAQ lists on Infoseek Guide include a hyperlink to each hit, the URL of the entire FAQ list, the FAQ archive name, and the frequency of posting the FAQ on the newsgroup.

Usenet FAQ   http://www.cis.ohio-state.edu/hypertext/
                                 faq/usenet/FAQ-List.html

Usenet FAQ provides text of the FAQ lists of many newsgroups, alphabetically. It has limited search capabilities as well, checking matches of your entered keywords against the newsgroup and archive names, subjects, and keywords identified for the newsgroup itself.

Searchable   http://www.lib.ox.ac.uk/internet/news/
FAQ Archive

This service of Oxford University Libraries is designed to perform keyword searches of Archived Frequently Asked Question files to get answers to commonly asked questions. FAQs can be searched by category, by newsgroup, or within each archive.

Another option is to perform a keyword search of newsgroup names to aid in the identification of newsgroups that match particular interests. There are several tools that make that type of search possible.

Find   http://www.cen.uiuc.edu/cgi-bin/find-
Newsgroups   news

Find Newsgroups is a searchable index of newsgroup names to aid in finding newsgroups of interest. A single character string is required (no spaces). The names and descriptions of newsgroups are searched to match the keyword entered.

Tile.net News   http://tile.net/news/

Tile.net News provides a substantial alphabetical subject index of Usenet Newsgroups, as well as an alphabetical list by description and by Usenet hierarchy. Keyword searches are available for any of the three lists.

Usenet Info Center Launch Pad	http://sunsite.unc.edu/usenet-b/home.html

From this location, one can access keyword search capabilities of all newsgroups to identify newsgroups of interest. This site also contains newsgroup FAQ lists.

If you're not looking for a newsgroup to monitor on an ongoing basis, but are trying locate newsgroup articles that might relate to a specific topic and could have been posted in any of several Usenet newsgroups, the entire universe of past Usenet newsgroup articles can be keyword searched. There are several engines that can accomplish this task, each taking a slightly different approach to the search process. There is also a tool which will allow you to monitor all Usenet newsgroups simultaneously and email posted articles which contain specific keywords to you.

Alta Vista	http://www.altavista.digital.com/cgi-bin/query?

Alta Vista can be configured to perform keyword searches across all Usenet newsgroups. This engine allows for the Boolean expressions "and", "or", "not", and "near" through the use of symbols included with the keywords. It also allows the searcher to require that some words be together in a phrase by surrounding them with quotation marks. Alta Vista allows the searcher to constrain newsgroup searches by entering restrictive requirements for *from:*, *subject:*, *newsgroups:*, *summary:*, and *keywords:* attributes and thereby limits the results of the search to articles that match those characteristics. Search results are provided in a compact form, just listing the site title and a brief description, or in a detailed form, which provides a brief description, the URL, and the document size.

Infoseek Guide   http://guide.infoseek.com/

Infoseek Guide offers keyword searches of Usenet newsgroups. Newsgroup searches provide results which include a list of hits in order of relevance. For each hit, the first two lines of the article are provided with a hyperlink to the entire article. In addition, hyperlinks to the newsgroup and to similar articles are provided.

DejaNews   http://www.dejanews.com/

DejaNews conducts keyword searches across all Usenet newsgroups. For each hit, it provides the subject header and sender in a hypertext format. Clicking on the header will give you the entire text of the article. Clicking on the sender will provide information about the Usenet practices of whomever posted the article, including other newsgroups in which he/she has posted, and the type of articles posted (original queries versus responses to the queries of others). DejaNews allows up to a maximum of 120 hits, allows the Boolean "and" and "or" to make keyword searches more specific, allows for filtering out undesired newsgroups, and allows the user to specify a preference for newer or older articles.

Excite   http://www.excite.com/

Although Excite is a well-known search engine for WWW pages, it also offers the capability of searching Usenet. The subject headers of hits are provided as hyperlinks. Clicking on one brings up the entire article. The article has a hyperlink for the sender, which when clicked brings up a "mailto" form for emailing that person. The newsgroup name is also hyperlinked and clicking on it brings up that Usenet newsgroup. Excite search results are listed in order of confidence that the hit matches what was specified. Clicking on the icon in front of a particular hit initiates a new search for similar articles.

Sift	http://sift.stanford.edu/

Sift, a news filtering service from Stanford University, allows you to design a profile of the type of Usenet articles you want. It then monitors the Internet continuously, and creates a web page of your hits or emails them directly to you. This is particularly useful if you are trying to keep abreast of Internet communication about a particular topic.

Searching Mailing Lists

Searching for a particular mailing list, or trying to find one that meets your needs, can be accomplished through several approaches. One approach is to search the content of newsgroups on a similar topic to see if any mailing lists on related topics have been discussed. The FAQ for a newsgroup might also might also contain information on related mailing lists. Another approach would be to post a query to a newsgroup, requesting information on mailing lists that are relevant to that topic or even narrower in scope. These approaches may provide information regarding mailing lists that aren't as widely known and may be impossible to locate elsewhere.

There are also several search tools to help identify mailing devoted to specific topics. Given the quantity and nature of mailing lists, however, no data base is very likely to contain a comprehensive list.

Mailbase	http://mailbase.ac.uk/welcome.html

A listserver for many lists in the UK, Mailbase has an alphabetized index of available mailing lists to help identify those of interest. FAQ lists are also available, as are searches by members' names.

Inter-Links Search List of Discussion Groups	http://www.nova.edu/Inter-Links/cgi-bin/lists

Inter-Links is a searchable database of over 5900 Bitnet and Internet Interest Groups maintained at Dartmouth College. Search results include the list's address, the list server's address, and the list owner's name and address.

Liszt	http://www.liszt.com/

A directory of over 20,000 listserv, listproc, majordomo and independently managed mailing lists from 617 different servers. Boolean "and", "or", and "not" are allowed to provide more specific direction to the search. Results include hyperlinks to information about each mailing list identified .

Tile.net Search Listserv	http://tile.net/listserv/viewlist.html

Tile.net Search Listserv provides alphabetical listings of mailing lists by their description, list name, host country, and sponsoring organization. It also allows keyword searches by subject of the entire data base.

Search for Mailing Lists	http://www.ucssc.indiana.edu/mlarchive/

Indiana University's database of over 12,000 mailing lists includes mailing list titles and official descriptions. The database can be keyword searched to match keywords assigned to each mailing list. Results provide the command and address to obtain information about the mailing list.

Searching for individual postings to mailing lists requires a search of the archives of the mailing list of interest. The location of the archives, if available, will be described in the list's FAQ list, or could be requested in a post to the list.

Searching Gopher

Gopher sites will sometimes be included with the results of web searches, but it is often desirable to browse likely Gophersites for information or perform keyword searches that are exclusive to Gopherspace.

Gopher Jewels   http://galaxy.einet.net/GJ/index.html

Gopher Jewels is a subject catalog of Gopher. It catalogs many Gopher sites by categories (58 categories, from agriculture and forestry to travel information). Clicking on a category provides a hyperlink list of all the topics within the category. Clicking on a topic takes you to the Gopher menu at that particular site.

Veronica   gopher://veronica.scs.unr.edu:70/11/
                                veronica

Veronica (**V**ery **E**asy **R**odent-oriented **N**et-wide **I**ndex to **C**omputerized **A**rchives) is *the* search engine for Gopherspace and provides access to resources held on over 99% of the world's Gopher servers. Veronica searches seek to match your keywords with the words in the titles of documents. Veronica searches also allow Boolean expressions. There are 10 public Veronica servers. Often one will be too busy to connect, requiring you to either wait or select another. Extensive instructions on composing Veronica queries can be found at:
  gopher://gopher.scs.unr.edu:70/00/veronica/how-to-query-veronica

---

Searching the Web

As the fastest growing area of the Internet, the web can provide a significant challenge to locate what can truly be a needle in a haystack. Web pages can be searched in several ways. One is by using a structured index or library that facilitates browsing by organizing sites in categories.

These indexes can be navigated by browsing through the categories until finding the desired resource. The web can also be searched by using keyword searches with search engines that contain databases of millions of documents.

Indexes and Catalogs

Using indexes won't likely provide the most exhaustive search, but may take you to sights you wouldn't identify with a keyword search. There are also sites which pull together many links related to a specific topic. Finding these "links" pages can save a tremendous amount of time.

Galaxy	http://galaxy.einet.net/

Galaxy offers major topic headings of business and commerce, community, engineering and technology, government, humanities, law, leisure and recreation, medicine, reference and interdisciplinary information, science, and social sciences. Major topics are sub-divided into numerous more narrow categories.

Master Web Server Directory	http://www.w3.org/hypertext/Data Sources/WWW/Servers.html

The Master Web Server Directory contains an alphabetical listing of registered WWW servers, by continent, country, and state. Data is also available by subject, by Library of Congress Classification, and by other protocols.

**Planet Earth
Virtual Library**

http://www.nosc.mil/planet_earth/
everything.html

The Planet Earth Virtual Library offers an extensive structured "virtual library" accessed via an image map. The image map is structured by major topic headings. Under each topic heading are sites to explore. It includes major categories of education, government, searches, science, etc.

**Virtual
Tourist**

http://www.xmission.com/~kinesava/
webmap/index.html

The Virtual Tourist is a map-based directory of WWW servers around the world. Rather than being organized by topic, the Virtual Tourist organizes sites by location. If the topic of interest is more geographically-based than subject-based, this is an excellent place to start.

Yahoo

http://www.yahoo.com/

Yahoo is one of the most popular indexes. It is discussed later as it relates to keyword searches, but also has a structured hierarchical index that can be browsed quite easily. It is organized around an extensive set of categories, subcategories, etc.

**The Whole
Internet Catalog
Select**

http://gnn.com/wic/wics/index.html

WIC Select is a large subject-oriented index with the following general categories: Arts & Entertainment, Business, Computers, Daily News, Education, Internet, Government & Politics, Sciences, Health & Medicine, Humanities & Social, Life & Culture, Personal Finance, Recreation & Sports, Science & Technology, Travel. This index does not claim to cover major portions of the Internet, but rather is quite selective in the sites it includes.

Keyword Search Engines

Just like a card catalog or periodicals index leads you to what you want in a library, a web search engine can lead you to what you want on the Internet. You enter keywords of interest, the search engine gives you the names of appropriate sites, URL, and maybe even some additional information. Keyword searches will provide you with the most extensive sets of URLs for any topic of interest.

The first thing to recognize about search engines is that unless someone submits a URL to be added to a search engine's list, or the engine's robot finds it on its own, the engine will not be able to find it when you run a search. Registering a site isn't always a quick process, so it is not at all unusual for the developer of a site to not submit it or to submit it to only one or two search engines. Because of the rapid growth of the Internet, it may also take several weeks from the time a site is submitted until it is actually listed. Search engines use different approaches to build their listings. Some start with a few known sites and, using "spiders" or "robots," examine all links from that set, and then examine all links from those, and so on, in a continuous process of finding new links. Others rely almost entirely on submissions.

Don't assume that a search on one engine is sufficient. Many of the search engines claim to have access to the most sites, the most users, and to be the best. Obviously, they can't all be the best. They are all quite good, but they aren't the same. They each have strengths and weaknesses. For one particular search a certain engine may give the best results. For another search the best results might come from a different engine. If you're really serious about finding as much as possible on a topic, you'll need to run several searches on each of several different search engines. Don't fail to keep in mind that there are lots of sites that have never been submitted to a search engine or are too new to have been found by robots. If you do find a site that fits your needs closely, explore it, because it may provide links to sites not likely to be found through a keyword search.

Most, but not all, web search engines allow keyword searches and Boolean expressions to be used together to provide the most specific search directions possible. This is particularly necessary when searching the web, where a search on one keyword can yield tens of thousands of hits. The Boolean expressions of "and", "or", and "not" allow the searcher to direct the engine to find pages in which *any* of a group of words is present or pages that contain *all* of the keywords. "Not" used prior to a keyword allows the search to exclude all sites that contain that word.

Some of the more popular search engines are listed below, in Table 3.1, and are briefly described in the section that follows.

Table 3.1: Some Popular Search Engines

Name	URL
ALIWEB	http://web.nexor.co.uk/public/aliweb/doc/ introduction.html
Alta Vista	http://www.altavista.digital.com/
Galaxy	http://galaxy.einet.net/
Excite	http://www.excite.com/
InfoSeek	http://www2.infoseek.com/
Inktomi	http://inktomi.berkeley.edu/query.html
Lycos	http://lycos.cs.cmu.edu/
Open Text	http://www.opentext.com/
Webcrawler	http://webcrawler.com/
WWW Worm	http://wwwmcb.cs.colorado.edu/home/ mcbryan/WWWW.html
World Access	http://www.infohiway.com/
Yahoo	http://www.yahoo.com/

ALIWEB	http://web.nexor.co.uk/public/aliweb/ aliweb.html

The ALIWEB information base depends on submissions of pages. ALIWEB keyword searches can be directed toward several record types, including the organization, document, service, user, or any combination. Options for the field searched include the title, description, keywords, or the URL. Options for the display of the results range from the titles only to the titles, descriptions, keywords and URL.

Alta Vista   http://www.altavista.digital.com/

Alta Vista offers the capability of searching the WWW or over 13,000 newsgroups. Search options include a simple query option that just uses keywords and an advanced query option that allows the use of "and", "or", "not", and "near". Search results are provided in a compact form, just listing the URL, site title as a hyperlink, and the first few words from the text of the document, or in a detailed form, which provides the URL, the site title as a hyperlink, the first three lines of text from the document, and the document size.

Galaxy   http://galaxy.einet.net/

Galaxy searches allow for Boolean expressions or a simple "check" of a box for finding "all" or "any" of the keywords. Search options include searching all of the text of the site, the title only, or the link only. Searches can also be directed to include Gopher or Telnet resources. Search results are available in three options. "Short" returns merely a list of URLs. "Medium" returns URLs, a relevance score, and an excerpt from the page. "Long" includes the URLs, a relevance score, an excerpt from the site, a brief outline from the site, and a count of the most frequent words (other than your keywords) in the site.

Excite   http://www.excite.com/

Excite differentiates itself from other search engines in a couple of ways. First, in addition to the typical searches which are based on matching keywords to documents which contain those words, Excite allows for "concept-based" searching. Concept-based searches will identify sites that match the concept, but might not be identified in a keyword search because they might not contain the exact keywords. Excite also allows for searching recent newsgroup postings. Excite does not utilize Boolean expressions. Results of Excite searches are presented with a summary, a score indicating the probability of the site being relevant to the search, and a red icon to designate those sites with the highest confidence. Clicking on the icon next to a particular hit will start a search for similar documents.

Infoseek   http://www2.infoseek.com/

Infoseek uses its own syntax to provide users with the ability to control their searches. Included in their search capabilities are ways to indicate words that should be close together, words that must be next to each other, words that should not be in the document, and other words that must be in the document. Boolean expressions are not supported. Hits are provided with a short abstract about the site. Infoseek limits results to 100 hits.

Inktomi   http://inktomi.berkeley.edu/query.html

Inktomi searches allow for the use of the Boolean "or" and "and" by placing a + or - before a word and allows up to ten words in a query. Inktomi ignores words that have fewer than three letters. Search results can be specified as being terse text, text only, or full graphics. "Terse text" provides the site title as a hyperlink and the number of occurrences of the keyword. "Text only" adds the URL to the results. "Full graphics" merely adds a row of dots as an indicator of relevance. Search results are presented as the title of the site, the URL, and a relevance score. Abstracts or descriptions are not returned with the search results.

Lycos   http://lycos.cs.cmu.edu/

Lycos (from Lycosidae, a family of large spiders which catch their prey by pursuit rather than by webs) searches the WWW, Gopher, and FTP sites daily, and collects information about each site including the text outline and the number of times the site is referenced by other sites (an indicator of the site's popularity). The results of searches are presented in order of the likely relevance of the site to your keywords and in order of site popularity. A site outline, abstract, and relevance score is provided for each hit.

Open Text   http://www.opentext.com/

Open Text searches provide options of finding the keywords in the site summary, title, first heading, URL, hyperlink, or anywhere.   Three types of searches are possible. *Simple searches* allow for the Boolean "or" and "and" or a search for a specific phrase. *Power searches* make it possible to find keywords using the same location options as the simple search, but add the ability to add the Boolean "not", a mechanism for identifying other words that should be near the keyword, or words that should follow it. *Weighted searches* add the ability to weight the results by a count of the occurrences of the keywords to the capabilities of the power search. Search results include a brief description of the site and options to visit the page, see the matches on the page, or find similar pages.

Webcrawler   http://webcrawler.com/

Webcrawler allows searchers to search for "any" or "all" of the keywords entered, equivalent to the Boolean "or" and "and" logic. Webcrawler does not provide an abstract or description of each hit, but does provide a "score" as an indicator of the likely relevance of the site. This score is computed by counting the number of times each of the keywords appears in the document and dividing that by the number of words in the document. The site with the highest ratio is given a score of 100. The scores for other sites are scaled to the best site.

WWW Worm   http://wwwmcb.cs.colorado.edu/home/
                                mcbryan/WWWW.html

The WWW Worm allows for using the Boolean "and" and "or" and a choice of searching for keywords in all URL references, in all URL addresses, only in document titles, or only in document addresses. Results include the title of the site and the URL.

World Access Internet Navigator	http://www.infohiway.com/

The World Access Internet Navigator provides access in an index form to the Web by country, topic, or by Web page title or owner. It also provides keyword search capabilities of the Web, Gopherspace, and ftp sites. Results of keyword searches include a brief description, keywords that apply to the site, and the URL.

Yahoo	http://www.yahoo.com/

Yahoo is one of the most popular indexes, not only because it has the capability of keyword searches, but also because it is a hierarchical index that can be browsed quite easily. It is organized around an extensive set of categories, subcategories, etc. Yahoo permits the use of Boolean "and" and "or" in keyword searches. Searches can look for the keyword(s) in the title, URL, or in the comments entered when a site is submitted for inclusion in Yahoo. Results are presented organized by Yahoo categories.

A Simple Comparison

To demonstrate how different these search engines are, the results of a simple comparative test are presented below in Table 3.2. Four searches were performed on each search engine. The engines were used in as similar a manner as possible to provide a good basis for comparison. If the Boolean "and" was needed, it was used whenever possible. Keywords were the same for each. The maximum amount of material was searched in each case; in other words, if the engine had options for searching just the title, or the URL, or the complete text, the broadest option was used. Searches were done on the following topics:

Leadership **and** team
Labor **and** unions **and** law
Inventory **and** reduction
Competitive **and** core **and** competencies

Table 3.2   Results of a Search Engine Comparison

Search Tool	Number of Hits			
	Leader and Team	Labor and Unions and Law	Inventory and Reduction	Competitive and Core and Competence
ALIWEB*	100	350	34	43
Alta Vista**	40,000	10,000	8,000	1,000
Galaxy	80	0	7	2
Excite*	>100	>100	>100	>100
InfoSeek***	100	100	100	100
Inktomi*	>200	>200	>200	>200
Lycos	809	4	54	0
Open Text	5,365	2,950	1,036	339
Webcrawler	1,460	241	139	13
WWW Worm	11	0	8	0
World Access	1	0	1	0
Yahoo	10	2,950	1,036	339

* does not provide a count
** provides an approximate count of sites which contain "some of the keywords"
*** limits results to 100 hits

This comparison is not meant to show that one engine is better than another, because the number of hits is not necessarily a valid measure of performance. The number of hits *that match what your are looking for* is what really matters. This small comparison does, however, show that these engines have access to different sets of resources and use different search approaches. Some search the entire text, some search only the titles, etc. This is reason enough to search on more than one engine. Over time you will develop a bias toward one or two engines that seem to consistently work well for you. You will also develop your own search strategy that works well.

An Initial Strategy

Several pieces of advice will help you find as much information relevant to your topic as possible with a minimal number of hits. Usually, the more general the search, the greater the number of hits, but the more you have to sort through results manually to find exactly what you want. The fewer the hits, the more likely you've missed something of value, but the easier it is to actually check all of the URLs returned. A good strategy is to start rather generally on an engine that tends to give a large number of hits, until you find a very close match. Once you find a close match, use it to guide more selective searches. If you are using Excite or Open Text, you can then search for similar pages. Once you find combinations of keywords that work on one engine, try them on others. Spend some time exploring the first good match. Reading a site that closely matches your needs is likely to provide you with potential keywords, search strategies, or even Boolean expressions you hadn't thought of. It may also contain links to similar sites. This will allow you to refine your search directions and increase your search efficiency.

The decision tree provided at the end of this chapter below can serve as a guide to direct your searches toward the tools that will best serve your needs.

Other Special Search Tools

There are a number of other search engines designed for narrow or special use. Depending on what you are looking for, they may provide a much more direct route to the resources desired. Several that are applicable to management topics are briefly described below.

U.S. Federal Government Agencies	http://www.lib.lsu.edu/gov/fedgov.htm
A comprehensive index page of all federal government agencies in the executive, judicial, and legislative branches, as well as independent and quasi-official agencies.	

| **The Federal** | http://www.law.vill.edu/fed-agency/ |
| **Web Locator** | fedwebloc.html |

Sponsored by the Villanova Center for Information Law and Policy, the Federal Web Locator is the one place to stop if you're interested in any site the federal government might maintain. The sites are broken into six categories:

Legislative Branch	Judicial Branch
Executive Branch	Quasi Official Agencies
Independent Agencies	Non-Governmental
	Federally Related Sites

Open Market	http://www.directory.net/
Commercial	
Sites Index	

Open Market has over 20,000 commercial sites indexed. They can be browsed via an alphabetical listing, or keyword searched. Keyword search capabilities include Boolean expressions. Results include the title of the site as a hyperlink and its relevant keywords.

World	http://wyp.net/search.html
Yellow	
Pages	

The entire yellow and white pages of the U.S. and Canada in one directory. Over 105 million listings can be searched.

Figure 3.1 Internet Search Decision Tree

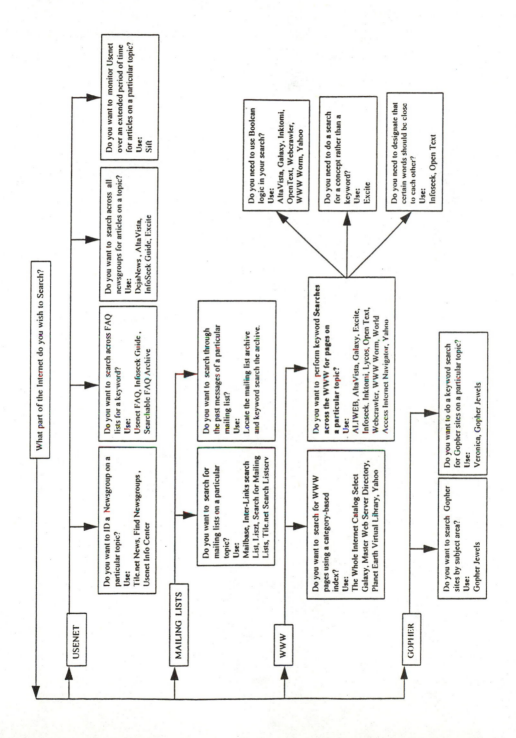

Chapter 4

Focus on Organizational Behavior and Management

This chapter provides specific focus on resources related to organizational behavior and organizational management. This broad topic has been broken down into the following topic areas:

General Organizational Behavior Sites
Conflict Management
Group Decision Making
Leadership
Learning Organizations
Motivation
Organizational Culture
Organizational Design
Teams
Mailing Lists
Newsgroups

General Organizational Behavior Sites

Management and Organization Research at Harvard Business School	http://www.hbs.harvard.edu/research/ summaries/mo.html

This site provides an overview of ongoing research projects at Harvard, related to the changing workplace; information organization and control; managerial behavior; negotiation; and teamwork.

The Management Archive	gopher://ursus.jun.alaska.edu/

This gopher site contains a variety of archived management resources, including calls for papers, teaching materials, working papers, management-oriented software, and others.

Organizational Issues Clearinghouse	http://haas.berkeley.edu/~seidel/ ad.html

The Organizational Issues Clearinghouse provides access to a mailing list which distributes calls for papers, conference announcements, etc. related to organizational issues. Current traffic on the list can be accessed through this site.

Organization and Management Theory	http://www.nbs.ntu.ac.uk/staff/ lyerj/list/hromt.htm

Organization and Management Theory is a "links" page providing access to a variety of Internet sites related to organizational behavior and organizational theory.

Business Communications WWW Resource Center	http://galaxy.einet.net:80/galaxy/ Business-and-Commerce/Management/ Communications/lance-cohen.html

This resource center provides some interesting practical advice on improving business-oriented communication. Included are suggestions for improving email correspondences, language improvement suggestions, other short articles providing practical advice and a few links to some other useful sites related to business communication.

The 60-second Issues Audit Questionnaire	http://vvv.com:80/mii/cia/

The 60-second Issues Audit is a 6-item questionnaire which, when completed, creates a rating of how well an organization is doing relative to such issues as safety and security, gender/ equity, and other issues.

Behavior Analysis Home Page	http://www.coedu.usf.edu/behavior/ behavior.html

This site is predominantly a links site for mailing lists, ftp sites, and related organizations.

OCIS Central
http://hsb.baylor.edu/fuller/ocis/

This is the home page of the Organizational Communication and Information Systems division of the Academy of Management. It offers information on the division, access to discussion lists, newsletters, etc.

Conflict Management

The Centre for Conflict Resolution
http://www.mq.edu.au/~ccr/

This center, located at Macquarie University in Australia, is devoted to academic research and teaching related to conflict resolution. Their newsletter is available online at this site.

Conflict Resolution Theory Building Centers
http://elan@csf.colorado.edu/../gb/
hewlett.htm

This site contains a comprehensive list of conflict resolution research centers located in the US. The list includes addresses, contact persons, etc. for each of the centers.

Conflict Resolution on the Internet
http://www.mq.edu.au/~ccr/internet.html

Conflict Resolution on the Internet is a "links" page of conflict resolution resources. Most are of an international affairs flavor, however, emphasizing issues related to conflict between countries, races, etc.

| **Conflict Resolution/** | http://www.coe.ufl.edu/CRPM/ |
| **Peer Mediation** | CRPMhome.html |

This site is the home page of a research center devoted to this topic. The page presents the purposes of the center, describes its projects, and provides links to several other CR/PM Internet resources.

Conflict	http://www.spcomm.uiuc.edu/projects/
Management	vta/vta021.402
Styles	

This resource is based at the University of Illinois at Urbana-Champaign Department of Speech communications. It provides a description of various styles of conflict management, including competitive, avoiding, accommodating, compromising, and collaborating styles. In addition to the detailed descriptions of each style, interesting examples are provided.

| **Conflict** | http://www.open.org/scserv/i6confli.html |
| **Management** | |

This is a link from the Community Involvement Home Page which provides an overview of issues related to conflict, help in understanding the nature of conflict, misconceptions, and managing conflict within a group. It is based primarily on two publications: Robinson, Jerry Jr., *Management in Community Groups*, 1976 and Wilson, Marlene, *Survival Skills for Managers*, 1981.

Group Decision Making

Group Dynamics and Group Decision Making Bibliography

http://mercury.hq.nasa.gov/office/ hqlibrary/ppm/ppm17.htm

This is a Program/Project Management List Resource from the NASA Headquarters Library. It provides an extensive bibliography of books and articles on small group decision making.

Collaborative Software Development Laboratory

http://www.ics.hawaii.edu/~csdl/

The Collaborative Software Development Laboratory, located at the University of Hawaii, pursues research in two areas. The first is research on software to enhance group activities, the second is research on developing software in group settings. The site contains information on the center's current projects, publications, and the people involved.

Consensus Decision Making

http://tdg.uoguelph.ca/~ontarion/users/ patti/consensus.html

This site, excerpted from the Ontario Public Interest Research Group (O.P.I.R.G) Working Group Guide, provides an overview of concensus decision making, particularly group conditions that support it.

Managing Effective Meetings	http://www.contrib.andrew.cmu.edu/ ~corona/meetings/meetings.html

This site provides guidelines for making meetings efficient and effective through a series of steps. Tools are described in detail with examples provided.

Leadership

Outdoor Action Group Dynamics and Leadership Program	http://www.princeton.edu/~rcurtis/ sect9.html

This site contains material from the Group Development and Leadership chapter of the <u>Outdoor Action Program Leader's Manual</u>, written by Rick Curtis. The primary topics covered in this site relate to Outdoor Action Leader Training Requirements.

International Review of Women and Leadership	http://www.cowan.edu.au/dvc/irwl/ welcome.htm

This is the home page of a journal published by Edith Cowan University (Australia). The site contains information about the journal, an index of past articles, calls for papers, and links to other women's resource sites on the Internet.

Leadership **Book Reviews**	http://www.stolaf.edu/stolaf/depts/ psych/leadership/reviews.html

This page contains reviews of a variety of books on various aspects of leadership. The reviews have been compiled by students in "Psychology of Leadership" courses at St. Olaf College.

LeaderAid	http://www.oise.on.ca/~bwillard/ leadaid.htm

This site is primarily a jumping off point for Internet resources on leadership and management development, but also offers some resources of its own. It includes links to other Web sites, conferences, books, papers, etc.

The Leadership **Home Page**	http://www-personal.umich.edu/~carlb/ leadership/leadership.html

This page, maintained by Carl Watson of the University of Michigan, contains several categories of resources related to the scientific study of leadership. Included is a list of leadership research centers, new books and articles on leadership, and his list of the "top ten" most important readings in the scientific study of leadership.

Leadership **and Organizational** **Development** **Journal**	http://www.mcb.co.uk/liblink/lodj/ jourhome.htm

This site is the home page of this journal and includes access to the journal's Internet conferences, calls for papers, editorial details, and articles, contents pages, and abstracts which can be browsed.

Jeff's Leadership Page	http://users.aol.com/leaderpage/index.htm

Jeff's Leadership Page consists of a set of pointers to a variety of leadership-related resources, including books and other WWW sites.

Total Leadership of Growth	http://www.connix.com/~tmac/leader.htm

A commercial page of the Michael Allen Company, but presenting some interesting perspectives on various specific applications of leadership, from a CEO's perspective.

Learning Organizations

Learning Organizations	http://www.ppress.com/productivity/ pp_learn_cat.html

This site contains excerpts from Learning Organizations, published by Productivity Press, including the full text of essays by Rosabeth Moss Kanter, Fred Kofman, and Peter Senge.

Center for   http://www.infi.net/~bclemson/
Organizational
Systems
Engineering

This is the home page of the center, devoted to learning, change
management, and high performance. Extensive descriptions of the
center's activities are provided, as are some links to other resources. The
research and activity of the center is predominantly from an engineering
management, rather than a behavioral, perspective. Thus, most resources
and methodologies are technologically based.

The Knowledge   http://www.iea.com/~bonewman/
Management   index-b.htm
Forum

KMF provides a source of interaction and discussion on topics related to
knowledge management. Several discussion groups are organized and
available. Bibliographies and reviews of related materials and links to
other sites are also provided.

A Bibliography   http://www.iea.com/~bonewman/
of Knowledge   bib_ey.htm
in Organizations

This site contains a very extensive alphabetical bibliography of
publications related to knowledge and organizations. Publications range
from the current back to the early 1980's.

Learning, Change, and Organizations
http://www.euro.net/innovation/ Management_Base/Man_Guide_ Rel_1.0B1/LCOrg.html

This site maintains an extensive set of resources, including access to references in the following topic headings: Quotes, Introduction, Change, The Need to Learn, The Learning Imperative, Assorted Papers on Organizational Learning, Modeling with Systems Thinking, and Soft Systems Methodology.

Learning Org-Dialog on Learning Organizations
http://world.std.com/~lo

This is the home page of an ongoing electronic discussion, LEARNING-ORG, which focuses on issues related to learning organizations. Current conversation traffic can be accessed at this site.

Knowledge Management and Organizational Learning
http://www.pitt.edu/~malhotra/ OrgLrng.htm

This is a direct link to the "The Knowledge Management Section" of *A Business Researcher's Interests*, which is a very extensive list of business-related resources. Many links are to specific articles related to this topic.

Information Management for the Intelligent Organization
http://www.fis.utoronto.ca/people/faculty/ choo/FIS/IMIO/IMIOpref.html

A virtual book, by Chun Wei Choo, containing extensive readings on information management within a learning organization.

Nijenrode's Research Center For Organizational Learning And Change	gopher://zeus.nijenrode.nl:70/11/About/ Departments/Research/Learning/

This center is a joint effort between several Dutch corporations and Nijenrode University. Its primary mission is to advance knowledge in organizational learning and change. Resources available at this site include case studies, information on seminars, course outlines, and descriptions of ongoing research at the center.

Stanford Learning Organization Web	http://www-leland.stanford.edu:80/ group/SLOW/

This site is maintained by a group of Stanford researchers, staff, and students interested in the topic of learning organizations. The site provides several lists of articles and books, particularly Senge's work.

Western Business School Organizational Learning	http://ashley.business.uwo.ca/~learning/

This site is maintained at the University of Western Ontario. It provides an extensive listing of papers and monographs on literature classification, theory development, and application, from the Western Learning Group.

Motivation

Employee Motivation and Empowerment Resources
http://www.saic.com:80/fed/motivation/

This site offers several short articles on culture, rewards, and bonuses. The articles are written by Matt Ward and Bob Nelson. Titles include:

> Creating An Ownership Culture
> Be Creative When Rewarding Employees
> Build Intrinsic Motivation into Your Incentive Programs
> Simple Gestures Count the Most
> Evolution of a Cash Bonus System
> Asset Appreciation Produces Best Returns
> Small Business Forum

Summary of Personality Typing
http://sunsite.unc.edu/personality/
faq-mbti.html

This site provides an extensive overview of personality typing, primarily focused on its application through the Myers-Briggs Type Indicator (MBTI).

Employee Motivation
http://mercury.hq.nasa.gov/office/
hqlibrary/ppm/ppm21.htm

This site is maintained by the Project Management Librarian at NASA Headquarters and provides an extensive list of articles and books related to employee motivation.

Organizational Culture

Surveying Organizational Climate Bibliography

http://mercury.hq.nasa.gov/office/
hqlibrary/ppm/ppm40.htm

This is a Program/Project Management List Resource from the NASA Headquarters Library. It provides a bibliography of books and articles which contain surveys that would be useful for an organization interested in surveying their organizational climate.

Studies in Cultures, Organization, and Societies

http://www.ucalgary.ca/~cancomm/
studies.html

This is the home page of the journal of the same name. It contains information about the journal, its goals, scope, etc. Descriptions of articles in current issues are available for browsing.

Pacific Region Forum on Business and Management Communication

gopher://hoshi.cic.sfu.ca:70/11/dlam/
business/forum

This gopher site contains a variety of resources related to management in different Asian cultures, including East and Southeast Asian, Chinese, Japanese, and Korean.

Organizational Design

Virtual Corporations
http://www.wordsimages.com/virtcorp.htm

This site provides brief descriptions of various aspects of virtual corporations, including their advantages, disadvantages, etc. It also provides links to a number of virtual corporations with Internet presence to show a variety of formats and examples.

Interorganizational Systems
http://www-iwi.unisg.ch/iswnet/index.html

This site provides links to resources addressing various issues related to information systems which cross organizational bounds. Included are articles and WWW resources in the areas of electronic commerce, electronic knowledge media, and technological fundamentals of interorganizational systems.

Transforming Organizational Structure
http://www.npr.gov/NPR/Reports/tosint.html

This is a direct link to the section of Vice President Al Gore's National Performance Review entitled "Transforming Organizational Structure." It is an in-depth analysis and description of issues related to the structure of the US Government and to productivity and performance improvement initiatives.

Inventing Organizations of the 21st Century

http://www-sloan.mit.edu/ccs/21c/prop.html

This site is maintained by a research center at MIT. The center's objectives are to answer questions related to the drastic changes which business organizations are having to face, particularly those related to downsizing, technological advancement, the necessity for rapid learning, needed changes in accounting methods, more rapid communication, and other issues.

Teams

Teams and Teamwork Bibliography

http://mercury.hq.nasa.gov/office/hqlibrary/ppm/ppm5.htm

This is a Program/Project Management List Resource from the NASA Headquarters Library. It provides a bibliography of books and articles on teams and teamwork .

Interpersonnal Relationships and Team Success

http://mercury.hq.nasa.gov/office/hqlibrary/ppm/ppm29.htm

This is a Program/Project Management List Resource from the NASA Headquarters Library. It provides a bibliography of books and articles related to interpersonal relationships and team success.

Ideas on Teams and Teamwork	http://www.oise.on.ca/~bwillard/ideateam.htm

This site provides access to a report from IBM, which details perspectives on teams and team management. Major headings include: Leadership, Power and Delegation; Teamwork and Teams; and Empowered Teams. Specific issues addressed include such items as: Leaders vs. Managers, Sharing of Information, Volunteerism, Empowering Others, Teams and Organizational Culture, Characteristics of Effective Teams, Team-player Styles, and more.

The Leadership Essay	http://vector.casti.com/qc/TQM-MSI/leadership.mfinley.txt

This is an excerpt from the book *Why Teams Don't Work*, written by Harvey Robbins and Michael Finley. It focuses on various aspects of leadership and their impact on team success.

Mailing Lists

General Instructions:

Unless otherwise noted, to subscribe to any of these listserves, send an e-mail message to the addresses listed below. Do not include a subject line. In the body of the email message type:

subscribe (listserve name) (yourfirstname) (yourlastname)

For example, if your name is "John Smith", and you want to subscribe to "LDRSHP ", send an email to "LISTSERV@iubvm.ucs.indiana.edu", leave the subject line blank, and type the following in the body of the message:

subscribe LDRSHP John Smith

A confirmation memo will be sent to your e-mail address. It will include instructions for sending messages to the list, how to unsubscribe from the list, and other important list-related information.

APP-ORGCOMM
Applied and Organizational Communication network
Learning organizations
To subscribe: send an email to majordomo@CREIGHTON.EDU
the following two lines:
        subscribe APP-ORGCOMM
        end
Do not include a subject. Do not include your name.

CCRNET
Conflict Resolution Network
To subscribe: listserv@alpha.acast.nova.edu

CMDNET-L
Conflict Management Division List
To subscribe: LISTSERV@KSUVM.KSU.EDU

COGNITION-IG
Managerial and Organizational Cognition Interest Group
To subscribe: LISTPROC@LISTS.COLORADO.EDU

Critical-Management
Discussion of research in the areas of business and organizational studies
To subscribe: send the command:
    Join critical-management firstname(s) lastname
to mailbase@mailbase.ac.uk

IABS-L
Social Issues in Management Division and International Association for Business and Society
To subscribe: LISTSERV@PSUVM.PSU.EDU

IOOB-L
Discussion List Devoted to Industrial/Organizational Psychology and
Organizational Behavior
To subscribe: LISTSERV@uga.cc.uga.edu

IT-TEAM
Management/Facilitative Leadership Forum
To subscribe: LISTSERV@CFRVM.CFR.USF.EDU

LDRSHP
Leadership issues
To subscribe: LISTSERV@iubvm.ucs.indiana.edu

LEADERS
Leadership training - Women in Leadership
To subscribe: LISTSERV@INDYCMS.IUPUI.EDU

Learning-Org
Learning organizations
To subscribe: send an email to majordomo@world.std.com and include
the following two lines:
>   subscribe learning-org
>   end
Do not include a subject. Do not include your name. Or see the contents
at http://world.std.com/~lo/LOinfo.html#stlo

Management-Research
Discussion of management research, its methodology, and development
To subscribe: send the command:
    Join management-research firstname(s) lastname
to mailbase@mailbase.ac.uk

OBTS-L
OB Teaching Society
To subscribe: listserv@bucknell.edu

OCISNET
Announcement & discussion list for the Organizational Communication
       & Information Systems Division of the Academy of Management
To subscribe: send a mail message to MAILSERV@BAYLOR.EDU.
In the body of the message include one line only, which says
SUBSCRIBE OCISNET.

ODCNET-L
Organizational Development and Change Division network
To subscribe: LISTSERV@PSUVM.PSU.EDU

OMT
Organization and Management Theory Division Archive
To subscribe: LISTSERVER@LISTPROC.STFX.CA

ORGCOMM
Communication in organizations
To subscribe: listserv@vm.its.rpi.edu

ORGCULT
Organizational Culture Caucus
To subscribe: listproc@commerce.uq.edu.au

RVL-L
Research on Visionary Leadership
To subscribe: LISTSERV@BYRD.MU.WVNET.EDU

TEAMNET
Teamnet research on teams.
To subscribe: send email to roquemor@terrill.unt.edu and in
the body include the following single line:
       join Teamnet

TEAMS-L
Quality Improvement Team Leaders and Facilitators
To subscribe: LISTSERV@UKANVM.CC.UKANS.EDU

The Organizational Issues Clearinghouse
Announcements of calls for papers related to organizational issues
To subscribe: follow instructions at
http://world.std.com/~lo/LOinfo.html#stlo

WIMNET-L
Discussion List for Gender Issues in Organizations
To subscribe: LISTSERV@VM.UCS.UALBERTA.CA

ZAPP
The Lightning of Empowerment
To subscribe: LISTSERV@UCSFVM.UCSF.EDU

Newsgroups

misc.business.facilitators
misc.business.consulting

Chapter 5

Focus on Human Resources Management

This chapter provides specific focus on resources related to human resources management (HRM). The broad topic has been broken down into the following areas:

General HRM Resources
Americans with Disabilities Act
Diversity in the Workplace
Employee Compensation and Benefits
Equal Employment Opportunity
Government HR-related Resources
Labor Relations
Safety, Health, and Ergonomics
Training and Development
Union Home Pages and Union-related Resources
Mailing Lists
Newsgroups

General HRM Resources

The Internet and HR: An Introduction
http://www.wp.com/mike-shelley/

For those not very familiar with the Internet, this page provides a useful overview of the Internet with links to several other HR resources.

The HR Professional's Gateway to the Internet
http://www.teleport.com/~erwilson/

This is the home page of Eric Wilson and contains numerous HR-related Internet links. Included are links to HR-related web pages, listserv information, and recruiting-related sites.

HR HQ
http://www.monster.com/hrnethome.html

For human resource professionals, HR HQ offers a gathering place and an informational resource. It includes several topic areas particularly related to recruitment, including listings of job fairs, layoff notices, recruitment advertising agencies, international recruiting suggestions, and more.

Industrial Relations: A Journal of Economy and Society
http://violet.berkeley.edu/~iir/indrel/indrel.html

This page contains information and abstracts from this US journal.

Human Resource Management & Organizational Behavior at Nijenrode's Gopher

gopher://zeus.nijenrode.nl:70/11/
Business/OBHR

This is a gopher site with links to several HR-related resources, particularly industrial psychology, organizational learning, and organizational change.

The Northern California HR Connection

http://www.hradvertising.com/
home_3.html

This site is a regional HR page which includes position advertising and an electronic bulletin board which allows HR professionals and students to post queries and responses about HR issues.

National Center for the Workplace (US)

gopher://uclink.berkeley.edu:3030/1

The NCW has goals of improving the competitiveness and performance of the American workplace by bringing together national leaders in business, labor, and government with eminent researchers to address workplace issues, and jointly develop public and private policies.

US Department of Labor Home Page

http://www.dol.gov/

This page provides links to the various department agencies (Sec. of Labor, Benefits Review Board, Bureau of Labor Statistics, etc.).

University of Michigan's Employment Statistics Gopher   gopher://una.hh.lib.umich.edu:70/11/ebb/employment

This gopher site contains various employment statistics and tables, including cost indexes, employment-unemployment statistics, collective bargaining settlements, unemployment statistics by state, etc.

HR Headquarters   http://www.hrhq.com/

HR Headquarters provides discussion groups on various topics, a conference room for networking, and a library with a variety of articles from *Personnel Journal.* The site requires a sign-up, but is free.

The Americans with Disabilities Act (ADA)

United States Department of Justice ADA Information Gopher   gopher://gopher.usdoj.gov/1/crt/ada

This is a gopher site, maintained by the US Department of Justice, devoted to the text of The Act, assistance manuals, frequently asked questions (with answers), myths and facts, enforcement status reports, etc., all available for review or download.

The Americans with Disabilities Act Document Center   http://janweb.icdi.wvu.edu/kinder/

This center provides links to numerous ADA resources, including sites concerned with specific disabilities such as HIV/AIDS, cancer, hearing impairment, visual impairment, mobility impairment, alcohol and drug-related issues, etc.

General Overview of ADA   gopher://personnel.ps.vt.edu:70/0F-1%3A749%3AGeneral%20Overview%20of%20ADA%20%28text%29

This site provides a short summary and overview (about 2 pages) of the Americans with Disabilities Act.

Americans with Disabilities Act-- full text   gopher://scilibx.ucsc.edu/11/The%20Library/Electronic%20Books%20and%20Other%20Texts/Americans%20with%20Disabilities%20Act

This Gopher site contains the table of contents, introductory material, and Titles I, II, III, IV, and V of the Americans with Disabilities Act.

Hospitality Industry Perspectives on Reasonable Accommodation   gopher://borg.lib.vt.edu:70/00/jiahr/92-09-08.jiahr

This is a paper from the Journal of the International Academy of Hospitality research, which addresses the essential components of reasonable accommodation for managers in the hospitality industry.

Diversity in the Workplace

University of Maryland Diversity Database

http://www.inform.umd.edu:8080/
Educational_Resources/Academic
ResourcesByTopic/Diversity

This database contains an extensive collection of diversity-related resources, including a reference room, issue-specific resources (age, class, gender, disability, national origin, ethnicity, religion, and sexual orientation), general resources, and more.

Administration on Aging

gopher://gopher.os.dhhs.gov/11/dhhs/
aoa/aoa

This is the US Department of Health and Human Services' Gopher site for aging-related resources. Included at this site are resources pertaining to the Older Americans Act, statistical profiles, an eldercare locator, health resources, a directory of state agencies on aging, etc.

Employee Compensation and Benefits

BenefitsLink

http://www.benefitslink.com/
home.htm

Benefits Link provides access to numerous resources related to employee benefits, including articles, government documents, benefits-related software, employment opportunity postings, and more.

American Compensation Association   http://www.ahrm.org/aca/aca.htm

This is the home page of an 18,000 member organization composed of practitioners, consultants and academicians who are engaged in the design, implementation and management of employee compensation and benefits programs. Information on events, seminars, professional certification, and publications is available.

At Work With Julie   http://netra1.abag.ca.gov/govnet/ julie/julie.html

At Work With Julie provides worker's compensation questions and answer's about the California worker's compensation system. It provides an entertaining and interesting Q&A system on specific applications of worker's compensation regulations.

Q&A About Worker's Compensation Insurance   http://www.consumer.com/consumer/ employercomp.html

This is a guide for employers, from the Massachusetts Executive Office of Consumer Affairs and Business Regulation. Issues covered include such issues as who has to have it, disputes with providers, costs, etc.

Federal Employee's Compensation Act   http://www.usgs.gov/feca/TOC.html

This resource is a U.S. Department of the Interior page on the FECA. It includes general information, commonly asked questions, and sections on: What if I am Injured?, Supervisor's Responsibilities, The Role of the Safety Officer, The Role of the Personnel Officer, and Penalties.

Entrepreneurs Guide to Guide to Equity Compensation

http://www.saic.com:80/fed/
guide/toc.html

This is a comprehensive resource, virtually a book online. Chapters
include: Developing and Equity-based Compensation Strategy, Stock
Purchase Programs, Stock Bonus Awards, Stock Option Plans, 401K and
Other Qualified Retirement Plans, ESOPs, Nonqualified Deferred
Compensation Arrangements, Simulated Equity Plans, Critical Issues,
Making Ownership Real, and supporting appendices.

Retirement Planning Associates, Inc.

http://www.insworld.com/Newsletter/
index.html

This is a commercial page that contains an index to *Benefits Insights,* a
nontechnical newsletter for managers who deal with retirement planning
issues.

The Clayton Wallis Compensation Site

http://www.crl.com/~clwallis/otherhr.htm

This compensation site is a links page providing access to a broad
spectrum of compensation-related Internet resources, including salary
indexes, professional associations, journals, etc.

Employee Benefits Education World Wide Web Site

http://www.ifebp.org/

This is the home page of the International Foundation of Employee
Benefits plans. The page provides an in-depth description of services and
resources offered by the Foundation.

Equal Employment Opportunity

Federal Civilian Employment Affirmative Action

http://www.whitehouse.gov/WH/EOP/OP/html/aa/aa08.html

This page provides an extensive review and evaluation of the effectiveness of Federal Affirmative Action Employment programs in several government agencies where they have been implemented. It begins with a history of the programs, describes implementations in a number of government agencies, and provides recommendations.

EEOC Guidelines on Preemployment Questions and Medical Exams

http://www.venable.com/wlu/pivec.htm

This resource offers employer-directed guidance related to EEOC obligations. Samples of lawful and unlawful interview questions are provided as a guide to employers concerned with appropriate interviewing procedures.

Handling Unlawful Questions

http://www.winway.com/pages/unlawful_questions.htm

For the interviewee, this site provides advice on how to react to, and answer, unlawful questions which might be asked during a job interview. It offers a list of topics which are generally not job related and offers examples of ways to effectively answer those types of questions that should not have been asked.

Government HR-Related Resources

U.S. Bureau of Labor Statistics
http://stats.bls.gov/blshome.html

This home page of the BLS provides access to time series data, news releases, surveys and programs, regional information, reports, and keyword searches of a collection of research papers by BLS authors. Copies of published and unpublished papers can be downloaded or obtained by mail. Abstracts for the Annotated Bibliography of Statistical Papers, the Economic Working Paper Collection, and the Current Population Survey Redesign Bibliography are available for searching.

U.S. Department of Labor Gopher
gopher://marvel.loc.gov/11/federal/ fedinfo/byagency/executive/labor

This extensive gopher site provides access to the Davis-Bacon Database (Via Fedworld), Bureau of Labor Statistics (BLS) Databases, Bureau of Labor Statistics (BLS) FTP Site, Consumer Price Index (Full Release), Employment Statistics, Occupational Outlook Handbook (From UM-St. Louis), Occupational Safety and Health Gopher Producer Price Index (Text and Tables), and the Federal Glass Ceiling Commission Report.

U.S. Securities & Exchange Commission EDGAR Database
http://www.sec.gov/edgarhp.htm

EDGAR, the Electronic Data Gathering, Analysis, and Retrieval system, provides automated collection, validation, indexing, acceptance, and forwarding of submissions by companies and others who are required by law to file forms with the U.S. Securities and Exchange Commission (SEC).

Labor Relations

A Primer in Labor Relations

http://www.globalone.net/lra/labor/union1.htm

This primer gives an overview of the key elements in the National Labor Relations Act. Written by Antone Aboud, Ph.D, this document would be of interest to students new to the field of labor relations and the NLRA.

Labor Policy Association

http://www.lpa.org/lpa/index.html

The LPA is an advisory organization of HR executives. The page provides links to current legislative issues, press releases, policy statements, voting analyses, and employment laws.

Cornell University's School of Industrial and Labor Relations

http://www.ilr.cornell.edu/

This Cornell site provides an extensive collection of resources including government reports (Downsizing, Glass Ceiling Commission, Child Labor, etc.), databases (Employee Benefits Infosource, etc.), and many publications from Cornell, including ILR Press, ILR Review, Institute of Collective Bargaining, and others.

Labor Relations
Web Picks
http://www.webcom.com/~garnet/labor/

This page contains an extensive list of Internet links related to
employment law, affirmative action/EEO, labor relations, personnel
management, collective bargaining, The Americans with Disabilities Act,
U.S. Supreme Court rulings on labor law issues, recent law suits, etc.

Developments
in Labor-Management
Relations
http://www.bls.gov/lmrhome.htm

This is a comprehensive site providing links to a broad range of resources
related to labor-management relations. Included are links to collective
bargaining settlements, bargaining activity, work stoppages, etc. Links to
various labor-management-related data sources are also provided. Related
resources, such as employment cost trends, safety and health statistics,
etc. are also made available at this site.

The American
Arbitration Association's
World Wide Web Service
http://www.adr.org/

Sponsored by the American Arbitration Association, this page is devoted
to alternative dispute resolution (ADR). It includes an introduction to the
association, a beginners guide to ADR, and current ADR news.

Venable's Labor
Law Upate
http://venable.com/wlu/wlu8.htm

This is a quarterly newsletter published by the Labor and Employment
Law Section of the law firm of Venable, Baetjer and Howard, LLP, of
Baltimore, MD. The newsletter addresses a broad range of labor law
issues. Prior issues back to January 1994 are available.

Safety, Health, and Ergonomics

Occupational Safety and Health Administration

http://www.osha.gov/

This home page of OSHA covers all aspects of the office. Included are publications, news releases, programs and services, OSHA standards, OSHA statistics, and more.

The Good Health Web

http://www.social.com/health/index.html

The Good Health Web is a general health-oriented resource page with information related to health-oriented organizations, discussion groups, a library of resources, health news, etc.

Index of Occupational Safety and Health Resources

http://turva.me.tut.fi/~tuusital/
oshlinks.html

This extremely comprehensive links page ranges from chemical safety to radiation to ergonomics to fire safety.

OSHA Compliance Assistance
http://www.osha.gov/compliance/index.html

This page is a service of the United States Department of Labor Occupational Safety and Health Administration. It includes an SIC Manual Search capability, references for most frequently violated OSHA standards, OSHA Field Inspection Reference Manual, and the OSHA Standards.

CTDNews Online
http://ctdnews.com/suffercare.html

From the Center for Workplace Health Information, this online publication devoted to cumulative trauma disorders (CTDs) presents the highlights from the actual publication. Included is information on CTDs in the workplace, government regulations, current topics from the news, etc.

ErgoWeb
http://tucker.mech.utah.edu/

From the University of Utah, ErgoWeb is a "jumping off" point for a variety of ergonomics-related information. Resources available through this link include: a vendor and manufacturer locator, analysis tools, case studies, OSHA guidelines and reports, and more.

Training and Development

TCM's Training and Development Home Page

http://iconode.ca/trdev/

A "links" page devoted to training and development issues and topics. This page contains links to the TRDEFV-L listserve and its frequently asked questions (FAQ) file, a listing of conferences, etc.

International Institute for Management Development

http://www.imd.ch/

From Lausanne, Switzerland, this page provides a summary of their programs, focusing on executive development from an international perspective.

Union Home Pages and Union-related Resources

A Union Guide to Computers

gopher://gopher.igc.apc.org/00/labor/ pubs/unionguide

A guide for unions wishing to utilize computers for word processing, accounting, bookkeeping, and other numerical analysis; to create databases for membership tracking; and to publish newsletters, flyers, and leaflets.

AFL-CIO **Organizing Institute**	http://www.aflcio.org:80/orginst/

As described in the home page, "The Organizing Institute was founded by the AFL-CIO in 1989 to promote and foster union organizing as a vehicle for social and economic justice. One of the first projects of the Institute was to recruit and train a new generation of union organizers."

Communications **Workers of America** **Labor Links**	http://www.wireless-apps.com/home/ links/index.htm

Home page of the Communications Workers of America.

The AFL-CIO **Home Page**	http://www.aflcio.org/

Home page of the AFL-CIO.

National Postal Mail **Handler's Union**	http://www.npmhu.org/

Home page of the National Postal Mail Handler's Union.

Service Employees **International Union**	http://www.seiu.org/

Home page of the Service Employees International Union

Sheet Metal Workers International Association	http://www.smwia.org/

Home page of the Sheet Metal Workers International Association.

United Mine Workers of America	http://access.digex.net/~miner/

Home page of the United Mine Workers of America.

Mailing Lists

General Instructions:
Unless otherwise noted, to subscribe to any of these listserves, send an e-mail message to the addresses listed below. Do not include a subject line. In the body of the email message type:
subscribe (listserve name) (yourfirstname) (yourlastname)

For example, if your name is "John Smith", and you want to subscribe to "UNITED ", send an email to "united-request@cougar.com", leave the subject line blank, and type the following in the body of the message:

subscribe LABNEWS John Smith

A confirmation memo will be sent to your e-mail address. It will include instructions for sending messages to the list, how to unsubscribe from the list, and other important list-related information.

AFFAM-L
Affirmative action discussion list.
To subscribe: listserv@cmsa.berkeley.edu

BENEFITS-L
Academics and practitioners in employee benefits.
To subscribe: listserv@frank.mtsu.edu

CAREERNET
Career Research & Management
To subscribe: listproc@credit.erin.utoronto.edu

COLLBARG
Collective bargaining for librarians
To subscribe: listserv@cms.cc.wayne.edu

CUPA-COMPSIG
College & University Personnel Assn.
To subscribe: listserv@carbon.denver.colorado.edu

EU
European Union Network
To subscribe: listproc@knidos.cc.metu.edu.tr

FLEXWORK
An e-conference on Flexible Work Environments
To subscribe: listserv@HMC.PSU.EDU

FUTUREWORK
Re-designing work, income distribution, and education.
To subscribe: listserv@csf.colorado.edu

H-LABOR
Labor history.
To subscribe: listserv@uicvm.uic.edu

HRD-L
Human Resource Development List.
To subscribe: listserv@mizzou1.missouri.edu

HRIS-L
Human Resources Information (Canada).
To subscribe: listserv@vm.ucs.alberta.ca

HRNET
Human Resources Division of the (American) Academy of Management.
To subscribe: listserv@cornell.edu>listserv@cornell.edu

HRNZ-L
HR in New Zealand
To subscribe: listproc@list.waikato.ac.nz

IERN-L
International Employee Relations Network.
To subscribe: listserv@ube.ubalt.edu

IOOB-L
Topic Information: This e-conference is for discussions of topics in the
fields of Industrial/Organizational Psychology and Organization Behavior.
To Subscribe: listserv@uga.cc.uga.edu

IRRA
Industrial Relations Research Assn.
To subscribe: listserver@relay.doit.wisc.edu

JOBANALYSIS
Job Analysis & Classification
To subscribe: listserv@listserv.vt.edu

LABNEWS
Labor union news.
To subscribe: listserv@cmsa.berkeley.edu

LABOR-L
Discussion group for international labor issues.
To subscribe: listserv@vm1.yorku.ca

NWAC-L
National Workforce Assistance Collaborative List.
To subscribe: listserv@psuvm.psu.edu

ODCNET-L
Organizational Development
To subscribe: listserv@psuvm.psu.edu

PAYHR-L
Pay & HR in Higher Education.
To subscribe: listserv@vm1.ucc.okstate.edu

PRIR-L
Pacific Rim Industrial Relations
To subscribe: listproc@list.waikato.ac.nz

PUBLABOR
Public sector unions and unionism.
To subscribe: listserver@relay.adp.wisc.edu

SOREHAND
Individuals who have an injury or disorder affecting the
hand/wrist/arm/shoulder/neck.
To subscribe: listserv@ucsfvm.ucsf.edu

STAFF-DEVELOPMENT
SD in Higher Ed.
To subscribe: mailbase@mailbase.ac.uk

TRDEV-L
Training and Development.
To subscribe: listserv@psuvm.psu.edu

UNION-D
European discussion list on labor unions.
To subscribe: leave subject line blank and type the following in the
message body: subscribe union-d (your email address), for example:
subscribe union-d jdoe@netcom.com

UNITED
Unmoderated list for anyone interested in the labor movement.
To subscribe: united-request@cougar.com

UNITE
U.S. Labor Network
ftpserver@cougar.com

WT-L
Working Together. A forum for those who want to share information about the realities of working together.
To subscribe: send email to majordomo@rain.org with "subscribe WT-L". Do not include your name.

Newsgroups

alt.discrimination
clari.news.labor
biz.general
biz.jobs.offered
misc.business.records-mgmt
misc.business.consulting

Chapter 6

Focus on Operations Management

This chapter provides specific focus on resources related to Operations Management. The broad topic has been broken down into the following areas:

General Operations Management Resources
Advanced Manufacturing Technology
Constraint Management
General Manufacturing
Just-in-Time
Management Science/Operations Research
Planning and Scheduling
Productivity Improvement, Business Process
        Redesign, Reengineering, etc.
Project Management
Purchasing and Logistics
Quality Management
Mailing Lists
Newsgroups

General Operations Management Sites

Information Innovation's Guide to Management and Technology	http://www.euro.net/innovation/ Management_Base/Man_Guide_Rel_ 1.0B1/Introduction.html

This is an extensive guide to technologies that interface with and are almost inseparable from management. This guide is a virtual book, in hypertext format, with extensive quotes and information on the following major topics: Artificial Intelligence, Change, Computing, Control and Monitoring, Databases, Economics, Finance, Financial Industry, Information, Innovation, Computing Knowledge, Management, Manufacturing, Marketing, The Networked Corporation, Open Systems, Policy, Reengineering, Strategy, Statistics, and Visualisation.

Warwick University's Operations Management Index	http://www.warwick.ac.uk/~bsryd/om/ index.html

This page consists of a comprehensive index of OM-related sites, including information on operations management, academic sites, conferences, mailing lists, OM literature, professional organizations, cases, working papers, etc. The site also includes an alphabetized hyperlinked index on many OM topics.

Information Innovation's Management and Technology Dictionary	http://www.euro.net/innovation/ Management_Base/Mantec. Dictionary.html

This site provides an extensive alphabetical dictionary of management and technology terms, concepts, famous individuals, etc. Business terms and concepts from the technical to the nontechnical are described and frequently supported with diagrams of models. Many definitions go beyond the brief overview to extensive descriptions.

OM-Info Access	http://www.muohio.edu/~bjfinch/ ominfo.html

OM Info-Access is maintained as a site to provide links to a variety of operations-related resources, including sites related to quality management, just-in-time, project management, planning and scheduling, constraint management, advanced technology, and other topics.

Journal of Operations Management	http://www.elsevier.nl/catalogue/SA4/425 /09405/09407/523929/523929.html

This is the home page of this research journal of the American Production and Inventory Control Society (APICS). It describes the journal's audience, scope, bibliographic information, where to get a copy, and presents the list of the editorial board.

Integrated	http://www.ie.utoronto.ca/EIL/
Supply Chain	iscm-descr.html
Management	

This is the home page of a research center which addresses issues related to the construction of supply chain intelligent agent systems. Publications available at this site include the following topics: Information Agents, Agent Shell Architecture, Coordination, Temporal Reasoning, Scheduling, Logistics, and Resource Management.

Advanced Manufacturing Technology (EDI, CIM, FMS, CAD/CAM)

Data	http://www.disa.org/
Interchange	
Standards	
Association	

The Data Interchange Standards Association (DISA) was charted by the American National Standards Institute (ANSI) to develop and maintain standards for the use of electronic data interchange. The site contains a broad range of EDI-related resources, Internet links, an FAQ list, job opportunities, etc.

| **Jim's EDI** | http://www.ibmpcug.co.uk/~jws/ |
| **Emporium** | index.html |

The EDI Emporium is essentially a "links" page, but also has some excellent introductory and more advanced documents on-site. Links go to EDI organizations, Internet sites, and mailing lists.

Electronic
Commerce
Resource Center

http://www.ecrc.gmu.edu/

This site provides information and resources in the areas of Electronic Commerce (EC), Electronic Data Interchange (EDI), Continuous Acquisition Lifecycle Support (CALS) , Enterprise Integration (EI) and Business Process Re-Engineering (BPR).

Electronic
Commerce
World Institute

http://www.ecworld.org/

The Electronic Commerce World Institute is an international non-profit institute whose focus is to accelerate the development and adoption of EDI and electronic commerce in business and government. This site is dedicated to information sharing and knowledge transfer. The site contains extensive information for beginners, including an FAQ list, an introduction to EDI, and an EDI glossary.

Academic
CAD Sites

http://www.kona.ee.pitt.edu/
AcademicCAD.html

This page provides links to a number of CAD-related sites. They are predominantly research labs and research centers at major universities.

Tampere University
of Technology
Production Engineering (Finland)

http://kiila.me.tut.fi/homepage.html

This site contains a variety of resources on CIM and FMS, including educational materials in the areas of manufacturing methods and automation and quality assurance techniques, including measurement and calibrations.

Flexible Ensemble Manufacturing

http://irobot.isi.edu/

This is the home page of an integrated supply-network scheduling project whose goal is to provide a higher level of software that bridges between local production information systems. The objective is to improve scheduling and inventory control in a manufacturing supply network. A paper describing the current status of the project is available.

McGill University's Center for Intelligent Machines

http://www.cim.mcgill.ca/

This center provides information on CIM-related research, directories, etc. Included at this site are resources related to their primary research objectives which are robotics and machine vision.

International Center for Research on the Management of Technology

http://web.mit.edu/icrmot/www/

This MIT research center is dedicated to research in technology management, specifically as it relates to business strategies, quality, optimizing product and process development times, manufacturing technology, etc. The site provides descriptions of projects related to these areas.

Constraint Management

Constraint Accounting Measurements	http://users.aol.com/caspari0/ toc/MAIN.HTM

This is a brief site on accounting aspects of constraint management. Some reports and short papers are provided.

Crazy About Constraints	http://www.lm.com/~dshu/toc/cac.html

This site contains an extensive collection of constraint management oriented resources. Included is background material, papers, notes, and information on related books and other materials.

General Manufacturing

Manufacturing Information Net	http://mfginfo.com/home.htm

MFGINFO provides access to manufacturing-related information, products, and services. There are also discussion groups on manufacturing issues.

Galaxy Directory of Manufacturing
http://galaxy.einet.net/GJ/mnfg.html

This Galaxy directory provides a list of links to a variety of manufacturing-related sites. Most are engineering and technology-oriented such as CAD, robotics, intelligent systems, etc.

The Thomas Register of American Manufacturers
http://www.thomasregister.com:8000/

The Thomas Register is an online "supplier/finder" of products and services for manufacturers. It is searchable by the product or service desired. Registration is required, but it is free.

Just-in-Time (JIT)

Western Australia's JIT Page
http://kernow.curtin.edu.au/www/ jit/jit.htm

This page is devoted to introducing and explaining JIT. It is a report, covering the following issues: What is JIT?, Planning for JIT, Requirements for JIT manufacturing, Critical elements in JIT manufacturing, Integrated Process Control, Detect Defects before they Affect..., Purchasing, Quality Control (QC), etc.

Poka-Yoke Page	http://www.cox.smu.edu/jgrout/pokayoke.html

This page is dedicated to the development of poka-yoke (failsafe, mistake-proof, error preventing) systems. It includes a poka-yoke tutorial, slides from several presentations on poka-yoke, and a readings list.

Inventory Management and JIT	http://wwwbs.wlihe.ac.uk/~jarvis/bola/jit/index.html

From the Business Open Learning Archive, this resource provides an overview of JIT, basic concepts, and specific information on Kaizen.

Management Science/Operations Research

Michael Trick's Operations Research Page	http://mat.gsia.cmu.edu:80/index.html

Michael Trick's page provides extensive resources in the area of operations research. It offers links to a variety of operations research sites and references including information on operations research-related journals, people, institutions, companies, institutions, courses, and jobs.

WORMS: Web on OR/MS
http://www.maths.mu.oz.au/~worms

WORMS was established by the Operations Research Group at the Department of Mathematics, The University of Melbourne, Melbourne, Australia. Its primary objective is to provide services complementary to those of the formal on-line activities of other OR/MS societies. It is in the preliminary stages of developing a Worms Virtual Encyclopedia.

Institute for Operations Research and Management Science
http://www.informs.org/

This is the home page of the Institute for Operations Research and the Management Sciences. It offers a number of OR-related resources including access to information resources, a searchable version of their membership directory, announcements about upcoming conferences, and searchable bibliographies of INFORMS publications and other OR/MS material.

Virtual OR/MS Library
http://www-personal.umich.edu/~msodhi/orms_lib/index.htm

This page provides links to a variety of OR-related resources including: Subject Lists (keyword searchable), OR/MS-related Societies and University Programs, Companies (Commercial), Government/Non-Profit Agencies, Conferences and Meetings, Electronic Journals, Online Bibliographies, Software, Test Problems for Math Programming, and more.

Planning and Scheduling

Forecasting Business Connection

http://weatherhead.cwru.edu/forecasting/

This page is dedicated to sharing information on business forecasting. It includes a forecasting FAQ list, results of research on forecasting, and information related to conferences, journals, etc. Discussion topics are also presented.

Artificial Intelligence Application Institutes Planning and Scheduling Group

http://www.aiai.ed.ac.uk/~pasg/pasg.html

This site contains resources related AIAI's focus, which is concerned with research and development of planning, scheduling and constraint management applications. Projects range from distribution logistics to manufacturing scheduling to project planning. This site contains descriptions of projects, papers, and planning and scheduling resources.

Scheduling-related Links

http://www.aiai.ed.ac.uk/~timd/
scheduling/

This resource provides pointers to a variety of scheduling-related links. Most are related to scheduling algorithms and heuristic tools of a technical nature.

Productivity Improvement, Business Process Redesign, Reengineering, etc.

Center for Productivity Enhancement	http://dragon.cpe.uml.edu/index.html

This is the home page for The Center for Productivity Enhancement (CPE), a research center at the University of Massachusetts at Lowell. Its goals are to improve the productivity of government, industry, and education. The Center's focus is on intelligent manufacturing.

What is Business Process Reengineering?	http://www.ecrc.gmu.edu/definition/bpr-define.html

This site provides an introductory overview and description of business process reengineering.

The BPR Home Page	http://ls0020.fee.uva.nl/bpr/

The BPR Home Page is maintained by the Reengineering Research Unit of the University of Amsterdam. It contains several BPR-related articles on BPR and descriptions of work in process at the research center. The site also maintains a list of other related Web sites.

Electronic College of Innovation

http://www.dtic.dla.mil/c3i/bprcd/index.html

The Electronic College of Process Innovation is a Department of Defense site which contains a comprehensive set of documents, tools and guidebooks on the topic of business process reengineering. Included are the following headings:

    Welcome New User, User Guide, Registration
    A guided tour of key concepts and documents
    Document listings, many with full-text online
    Software tools and utilities information
    Classes, training courses, and tutorials
    Reference documents on Acquisition Reform

WARIA

http://vvv.com/waria/

This is the home page of the Workflow and Reengineering International Association. The association's goals are to identify and clarify issues that are common to all users of workflow and those who are in the process of reengineering their organizations. Resources available at this site include materials available through the association, a database of vendors and consultants, and descriptions of association benefits and conferences.

Business Process Reengineering/ Innovation

http://www.pitt.edu/~malhotra/BPR.htm

This is the "BPR" area of Business Researcher's Interests, a comprehensive business resource site. The BPR list is one of the most comprehensive BPR resources on the Internet. It contains an extensive set of materials, articles, abstracts, and links to other BPR resources. Beyond BPR, it also contains resources related to workflow, groupware, etc.

Phoenix   http://www.phoenix.ca/bpr/bpr/Articles/
BPR
Articles

This site contains a set of articles available online. Articles range from
book reviews, to articles on general aspects of BPR, to literature reviews.

Business   http://raider.mgmt.purdue.edu:80/
Process   ~shashi/bpr/bpr.html
Reengineering

This resource offers a collection of links to a variety of sites related to
BPR, Workflow, Groupware, etc. General BPR links provide a
comprehensive listing of BPR sites, mailing lists, etc.

Project Management

The Project   http://www.wst.com/projplan/proj-
Management   plan.glossary.html
Glossary

The Project Management Glossary provides extensive explanations of a
large number of project management-related terms.

| The WWW Project Management Forum | http://www.synapse.net/~loday/ PMForum/ |

The Project Management Forum contains an extensive set of resources on project management, including references to books, careers, an event calendar, journals, magazines, new postings, a notice board, and professional organizations.

| The Project Management Institute | http://www.pmi.org/ |

This is the home page of this institute. It describes all services available through the institute, including publications, education and training, certification information and other services.

| Program and Project Management Resources | http://mercury.hq.nasa.gov/office/ hqlibrary/ppm/ppm.htm |

This site provides access to NASA's library of references related to Program and Project Management. The library contains over 40 extensive bibliographies on management-related topics.

Purchasing and Logistics

Advanced Procurement Systems Home Page
http://www.realtime.net/aps/

The Advanced Procurement Systems home page is devoted to automation in public purchasing. Major headings of resources include Basic Purchasing, Open Market, Contract Purchasing, Stock Inventory, Department Access, Electronic Data Interchange, Troubleshooting, and The NIGP Commodity/Service Code.

Managing Supplier Relationships
http://www.dbisna.com/dbis/purchase/vpurchas.htm

Managing Supplier Relationships is a commercial site offering some interesting tips and suggestions on managing supplier relationships, including qualifying suppliers, and tracking supplier performance.

LogLink
http://www.commerce2000.com/logistics/loglink.htm

LogLink is an extensive links page for resources directly and indirectly related to business logistics. In addition to logistics, it includes a broad spectrum of more general business-related links. Links are indexed by category.

An Introduction to Supply Chain Management	http://silmaril.smeal.psu.edu/misc/ supply_chain_intro.html

This site provides an introductory description of Supply Chain Management, including decisions related to location, production, inventory, transportation, supply chain modeling, network design, and rough-cut methods.

NAPM Home Page	http://www.napm.org/napm.html

This is the home page of the National Association of Purchasing Management, a professional organization of over 38,000 purchasing and supply management professionals. The site houses information on the organization, certification processes, and educational resources available from the organization.

International Logistics	http://www.commerce2000.com/ logistics/woklcou.htm

International Logistics is an index, by country, of logistics-related information and resources. Global resources available at the site include roads, ships, ports, rail, logistics and transportation agencies, research, and more.

Quality Management

General Quality Sites

QualiNet	http://www.qualinet.com/

QualiNet provides links to other quality-related resources, a virtual conference room for electronic discussions, and a "networking" aid for quality professionals.

Quality Management Principles	http://www.wineasy.se/qmp/

The Quality Management Principles page provides statements and definitions of quality management principles. Briefly, the principles are: Customer-driven organization; Leadership; Involvement of people; Process approach, System approach to management; Continual improvement; Factual approach to decision making. The principles are described and discussed from the perspective of the role they play in ISO9000.

Quality Resources Online	http://www.quality.org/qc/

Quality Resources Online is considered by many to be the "mother of all quality pages." It contains an extensive collection of resources and links covering a broad range of topics including virtually anything related to quality, from Deming to Dilbert.

The American Productivity and Quality Center
http://www.apqc.org/

The APQC is a not-for-profit organization offering various resources with the primary focus on increasing competitiveness. Education and training services include curriculum planning and course design, public seminars and in-house training, and licensing of training materials. Information services consist of research and reference services, a publicly-accessible research library of quality and productivity materials, and periodical and special publications. Benchmarking services include process improvement, benchmarking, and surveys. The APQC also houses the International Benchmarking Clearinghouse.

The American National Standards Institute
http://www.ansi.org/

This page is a link to official standards and standards-related information. It provides access to the standards information database (SID), which offers up-to-date information on standards-related activity throughout the world. It also provides access to the national standards system network (NSSN) with search capabilities, as well as extensive information on training and educational services, the ANSI catalog, and other standards-related resources.

American Society of Quality Control
http://www.asqc.org/index.html

This is the home page of the American Society of Quality Control (ASQC). It provides information on ASQC as well as access to a number of ASQC resources, including ASQC programs and services, quality related resources, and quality news.

The Quality Network (UK)
http://www.quality.co.uk/quality/

The Quality Network provides access to a variety of resources, including some related to quality management (consultants, Internet resources, benchmarking, configuration management), ISO9000, environmental management (ISO14000, training, consulting), safety management and other business-related services.

The Virginian-Pilot Online Inside Total Quality Management
http://www.infi.net/pilot/extra/tqm/

This page presents an article published by the Virginian-Pilot (newspaper) online version. It provides a comprehensive overview of TQM, its history, Deming's involvement, its impact on workers and their jobs, conflicts with U.S. culture, and expectations for its future.

Clemson's Continuous Quality Improvement Gopher Site
gopher://deming.eng.clemson.edu/

Clemson's CQI gopher provides four categories of CQI-related resources. It provides access to the files of the TQM bulletin board, it provides the archives of material from the community quality electronic network (CQEN), it acts as a repository for quality-related resources others wish to submit, and it offers support for CQI efforts within Clemson's College of Engineering. Three items on the gopher menu will be of most use. The Public File Area (CQEN, DEN and CQI Files) will allow for browsing among all of the files. Search CQEN and DEN and Search CQI File Areas allow for keyword searches.

Babson	gopher://vaxvmsx.babson.edu:70/11
Quality	gopher_root:%5bquality.archive%5d
Archive	

This gopher site provides links to other quality-related gopher sites as well as some resources related to quality. Among the resources are several papers, including "TQM and Malcolm Baldrige: A Practitioner's Approach" and "TQM in Higher Education: The Babson College Journey."

University of	gopher://gopher.adp.wisc.edu:70/11/.
Wisconsin	facstf/.tqm
Quality	
Gopher Server	

Wisconsin's Quality Gopher site contains information related to the IBM-TQM partnership with colleges and universities, the newsletter of the Madison Area Quality Improvement Network, and an extensive quality and productivity improvement report list. This set of papers and reports contains a very comprehensive set of resources, from technical reports to management-oriented reports to case studies.

Quality Tools and Techniques

Quality	http://mijuno.larc.nasa.gov/dfc/qtec.html
Technology	
Page	

Managed by Ed Dean, of NASA, the Quality Technology Page offers reference material on many of the tools and techniques associated with quality management. Included are resources related to: Design for Quality, Hoshin Kanri , ISO9000, Kaizen, Quality Function Deployment, Seven Basic (Old) Tools, Seven Management (New) Tools, Seven New Product Planning Tools, Statistical Quality Control, Taguchi Methods, Total Quality Control, and Total Quality Management.

Quality Function Deployment	http://mijuno.larc.nasa.gov/dfc/qfd.html

This page provides an overview of the QFD process with links to important components, such as the voice of the customer, the seven traditional quality tools, etc.

The QFD Institute	http://www.nauticom.net/www/qfdi/

This site is the home page of the QFD Institute and contains information about the organization, lists of resources available from it, and contains several quality function deployment (QFD) resources, and links to some other quality-related sites.

Process Benchmarking Links Collection	http://www-iwi.unisg.ch/iwi2/cc/ bm/links/index.html

This is a "links" page devoted to process benchmarking. Categories covered include Benchmarking Objects (business strategies, financial figures, process outputs, output creation, hardware/software, information systems), Benchmarking Partners (non-commercial, commercial, partners for comparison), Benchmarking Publications (case studies, how to do benchmarking.

US Department of Labor Best Practices Clearinghouse

http://www.saic.com/fed/uscompanies/labor/

This page is maintained by the Office of the American Workplace as a means of disseminating information related to the "best practices" used by high performance companies. An alphabetical listing of company profiles is provided. Company profiles offer company descriptions as well as detailed descriptions of practices in the following areas: training and continuous learning, employee participation, access to information, organizational structure, employment security, supportive work environment, product/service quality, compensation linked to performance, worker-management relations, and strategic integration of business.

Benchmarking

http://www.quality.co.uk/quality/benchadv.htm

This page consists solely of an article published by Peter Griffen. It provides a brief overview of benchmarking and includes discussions of selecting an object to benchmark, selecting a benchmarking partner, gathering information, performing a visit, using the information gathered, etc.

The Benchmarking Exchange

http://www.benchnet.com/

The Benchmarking Exchange is the home page of an organization which offers a comprehensive set of benchmarking resources. Members are able to access information related to the practices of "best-in-class" companies on a broad range of business processes.

Quality Awards and Certification

ISO14000 Standards	http://www.quality.co.uk/quality/eco/isolist.htm

This page contains the list of the ISO14000 series of environmental standards and links to other environmentally-oriented pages.

Quality Standards- ISO9000	http://www.mep.nist.gov/resources/iso9000/iso9000.html

This page contains the National Institute of Standards and Technology (NIST) resources on ISO9000. Included are keyword search capabilities of ISO9000-related documents, Q&A on ISO9000, statements of standards, registration information for ISO9000, and the Baldrige Award.

ISO Online	http://www.iso.ch/welcome.html

ISO Online contains a wide spectrum of educational resources related to ISO certification. Major topic headings include: Introduction to ISO, ISO technical committees, ISO structure, ISO meeting calendar, ISO members worldwide, and an ISO catalogue. An ISO9000 forum, with information on specific quality-related issues and a "What's new" section providing new information are also available at this site.

The ISO9000 Guide	http://www.ileaf.com/isoguide.html

The ISO9000 Guide is an extensive guide to the ISO9000 process, including the following major headings: Background of the ISO9000 Standard, The ISO9000 Registration Process, Document Management and ISO9000 Certification, ISO9000 Certification-Why So Many Organizations Fail, ISO9000 and Quality Systems, Why ISO9000 Benefits Your Organization, etc.

| ISO Certification Case Study | http://www.marinenetwork.com/ ~qualnet/.isocase1.html |

This site contains a detailed description of the successful ISO certification of an assembler of integrated circuits. The case is organized around key questions, with answers being descriptions of what this firm did. Key questions include such issues as what role the consultant should take, what actions were taken by the consultant, a strategy for cleaning up a major noncompliance, management actions while the consultant was not present, etc. Much of the case is described in almost a day-to-day diary format.

| National ISO9000 Support Group | http://www.cris.com:80/~isogroup/ |

This is the home page of an organization devoted to providing support to those firms pursuing ISO9000 or ISO14000 certification, with the goal of reducing confusion. Links to ISO9000 and ISO14000 resources are provided and offered free to students and those studying these topics.

| ISO9000 Forum | http://www.hike.te.chiba-u.ac.jp/ikeda/ documentation/iso9000/index.html |

ISO9000 Forum offers extensive resources related to ISO9000. References range from those that would be useful to someone not familiar, like "Getting Started," "Facts on ISO9000," or "24 Questions on ISO9000" to the advanced. Links to software related to ISO9000 are also provided at this site.

| O'logics ISO9000 Tools | http://www.Ologic.com/ |

This page provides an introductory overview of ISO9000 and a free evaluation copy of software which provides a quality manual template.

**National   http://www.nist.gov/quality_program/
Institute of
Standards and
Technology (NIST) Quality Information**

This is the home page of NIST and presents NIST resources related to
achieving ever-improving value to customers through the efforts of the
Baldrige Award. All official Baldrige Award-related resources are
available at this site, including information related to the healthcare and
education pilot programs.

**Baldrige   http://www.nist.gov:8102/doc/Win/
Award   ABOUT_QUALITY_AWARD_
Winners   WINNERS_1988_-_1994.html**

This is a direct link to the NIST pages devoted to each of the Baldrige
Award winners. Each company has a significant amount of information,
including company descriptions, information on their TQM efforts, even
photos.

**The Shingo   http://www.phoenixcg.com/shingo.html
Prize for
Excellence in
US Manufacturing**

This page is dedicated to the Shingo prize, and includes a brief history of
the prize, the mission of the Shingo prize, a description of the award
application process, the examination items and their point values, and a
brief biographical sketch of Shigeo Shingo.

Mailing Lists

General Instructions:
Unless otherwise noted, to subscribe to any of these listserves, send an e-mail message to the addresses listed below. Do not include a subject line. In the body of the e-mail message type:
subscribe (listserve name) (yourfirstname) (yourlastname)

For example, if your name is "John Smith", and you want to subscribe to "BPR-l ", send an e-mail to "listserv@is.twi.tudelft.nl", leave the subject line blank, and type the following in the body of the message:

subscribe BPR-l John Smith

A confirmation memo will be sent to your e-mail address. It will include instructions for sending messages to the list, how to unsubscribe from the list, and other important list-related information.

APN
Applied Probability Newsletter
To subscribe: Send request to Mike Bailey
mike@uwhiz.or.nps.navy.mil

ASQC-CSD
ASQC Customer-Supplier Division
To subscribe: send "subscribe asqc-csd" to majordomo@quality.org
Do not include your name or email address.

ASQC-MQD
ASQC Measurement Quality Division
To subscribe: send "sub asqc-mqd" to majordomo@quality.org
Do not include your name or email address.

BPMI
Business Process Management & Improvement
To subscribe: send "subscribe bpmi" to majordomo@quality.org
Do not include your name or email address.

BPR-l
Business Process Reengineering
To subscribe: listserv@is.twi.tudelft.nl

CQEN
Community Quality Electronic Network at Clemson University
To subscribe: Send the word "subscribe" (without quotes) in the subject
line to cqen.list-request@deming.ces.clemson.edu

CSP
Techniques of Constraint Satisfaction
To subscribe: listserver@saturne.cert.fr

DEN
Deming Electronic Network at Clemson University
To subscribe: Send the word "subscribe" (without quotes) in the subject
line to den.list-request@deming.ces.clemson.edu

EDI-L
General EDI discussions
To subscribe: listerv@uccvma.ucop.edu

EITF-EDI
Discussions on new approaches to EDI
To subscribe: listserv@byu.edu

ISO9000
Moderated discussion on ISO9000
To subscribe: LISTSERV@VM1.NODAK.EDU

MFG-INFO
Manufacturing topics
To subscribe: LISTSERV@MSU.EDU.BITNET

MOP-group
Measuring Organizational Performance
To subscribe: send "subscribe mop-group" to majordomo@quality.org
Do not include your name or email address.

NEW-EDI
Discussions on new approaches to EDI
To subscribe: edi-new-request@tegsun.harvard.edu

NEWPROD
New Product Development
To subscribe: send "subscribe NEWPROD to
MAJORDOMO@WORLD.STD.COM
Do not include your name or email address.

OPEN-EDI
Review the ISO approach to OPEN EDI
To subscribe: send "subscribe open-edi to
majordomo@utu.premenos.com.
Do not include your name or email address.

QFD-l
Quality Function Deployment
To subscribe: send "subscribe qfd-l" to majordomo@quality.org
Do not include your name or email address.

QUALITY
TQM in Manufacturing and Services
To subscribe: LISTSERV@PUCC.PRINCETON.EDU

Quality Management
To subscribe: send "join quality-management *yourname*" to
mailbase@mailbase.ac.uk

TOC-l
Theory of Constraints
To subscribe: listserv@netcom.com

TQMBBS
Total Quality Management Bulletin Board at Clemson University
To subscribe: Send the word "subscribe" (without quotes) in the subject
line to tqm.list-request@deming.ces.clemson.edu

TQM - Clemson
Total Quality Management
To subscribe: send "subscribe" to tqm.list-request@deming.
eng.clemson. edu

TQM-d
Total Quality Management
To subscribe: send "subscribe tqm-d" to majordomo@quality.org

TQMEDU-L
Total Quality Management in Higher Education
To subscribe: send request to TQMEDU-L@HUMBER

TQM - Kansas
Total Quality Management
To subscribe: listserv@ukanvm.cc.ukans.edu

TQM-L
Total Quality Management in Higher Education
To subscribe: send request to TQM-L@UKANVM

TQMLIB
Total Quality Management for Libraries
To subscribe: send request to TQMLIB@WAYNEST1

Newsgroups

alt.cad
alt.cad.autocad
alt.books.technical
alt.business.multi-level
misc.industry.quality
biz.config
biz.sco.general

Chapter 7

Focus on Strategic Management

This chapter provides specific focus on resources related to strategic management. This broad topic is broken into the following topic areas:

Business Plans
Business Ethics
Entrepreneurship
International Business
Small Business Management
Strategic Management
Mailing Lists
Newsgroups

Business Plans

Preparing a Business Plan
http://www.sb.gov.bc.ca/smallbus/workshop/market/prepare/busplan.html

This site contains a summary of how to prepare a business plan, written by a small business agency in British Columbia. It includes information on the following topics: Why Prepare a Plan?, Business Concept, Financial Plan, Approaching Lenders, and Attracting Investors.

Strategic Business Planning
http://www.dbisna.com/dbis/planning/vplannin.htm

This is a commercial site, but it contains one section, "Seven tips to help you create a business planning roadmap," which includes useful tips on creating business plans.

Sample Business Plan
http://www.sb.gov.bc.ca/smallbus/workshop/market/sample/sample.html

From the same British Colombia site, a hypertext sample business plan based on a fictitious small company. The plan is quite extensive, with all necessary sections presented to serve as a model for other plans.

Sample Business Plan	http://www.kciLink.com/brc/bplan/

This site, maintained by a software company, contains another sample business plan, created by business plan generating software. The business plan is for a fictitious consulting company and provides a nice outline and sample plan.

Smart Business Plan Resource File	http://www.smartonline.com/ netpage.html

A commercial site offering resources on developing a business plan. Major topic areas include: What is a business plan?, What is Smart Business Plan?, Why write a business plan?, What is the best format for a business plan?, What format does Smart Business Plan use?, Are there other sections I might include?, Are there complete example plans provided?, How do I decide what type of business I am? and Hints for business plan writers.

Business Ethics

Business Ethics Resources on the WWW	http://www.ethics.ubc.ca/papers/ business.html

Business Ethics Resources contains a broad set of ethics-related links ranging from papers, to resources on specific ethics-related topics, institutions, and organizations.

DePaul   http://www.depaul.edu/ethics/
University
Institute for Business
and Professional Ethics

This university site contains an extensive set of resources related to
business ethics. Included are links to many other resources, an online
journal, teaching resources, information about the institute, and
professional information (position vacancies, calls for papers, etc.)

Ethics on the   http://www5.fullerton.edu/les/
World Wide   ethics_list.html
Web

From the University of California--Fullerton, this is a comprehensive
listing of ethics-related resources which also contains a broad base of
more specific ethics topics such as computer ethics, environmental ethics,
legal ethics, media ethics, medical ethics, military ethics, etc.

Ethical   http://www.bath.ac.uk/Centres/Ethical/
Business

From the UK, this site is devoted to ethical investment and environmental
issues, predominantly investments which are sound from an
environmental ethic standpoint.

Nijenrode's   http://www.nijenrode.nl/nbr/eth/
Business Webserver on
Ethics, Environment and Sustainability

Nijenrode's site contains an extensive listing of Internet resources related
to these issues. Topic headings include ethics, business ethics,
environment, philosophy, and sustainability. References include business
lists, codes of conduct, etc.

Entrepreneurship

US Patent and Trademark Office
http://www.uspto.gov/

This government site contains an extensive guide to the Patents and Trademark Office, reference materials for people unfamiliar with patents and trademarks, a contact list for virtually all aspects of patent and trademark processes, a fee schedule, etc.

The Strategic Patent Web Site
http://www.pacificrim.net/~patents/

This site is maintained by a commercial patenting service and offers links to a variety of resources of interest. Included are drawing- and graphic-related links, an extensive set of patent-related Web sites, etc.

FAQs About Patents and Trademarks
http://salix.lib.washington.edu/libinfo/ libunits/sciences/engineering/ patents/faq.html

This site contains questions and extensive answers related to patents and trademarks. Topics include those related to the process of obtaining patents and trademarks, suggestions for obtaining more information, etc.

The Vine   http://www.thevine.com/

The Vine is the nome page of <u>V</u>enture <u>I</u>nformation <u>N</u>etwork for
<u>E</u>ntrepreneurs. Issues addressed and resources provided range from
finding capital, government links, showcasing entrepreneurs, emergent
growth opportunities, a reference library, and many other
entrepreheurship-oriented resources.

Home Business   http://www.tab.com/Home.Business/
Review

This is the home page of a newspaper devoted to owners of home-based
businesses. The page provides descriptive information of the various
services and features offered by the publication.

Nijenrode's   gopher://zeus.nijenrode.nl/11/Business/
Entrepreneurship   Strategic
Gopher

Like the other business resources at Nijenrode, this one contains some
useful resources. It provides a small business bibliography and two useful
small business guides: a small business guide to trade finance and a small
business guide to exporting.

Red Herring   http://gnn.com/wic/wics/bus.85.html

Red Herring is the home page of a magazine devoted to small, growing
technology companies and venture capitalists. An archive of back issues
can be accessed.

Association of Collegiate Entrepreneurs
http://www.csupomona.edu/ace/

This organization, headquartered at California Polytechnic University, provides this site. It provides information about the organization and links to related Internet resources.

Entrepreneurial Edge Online
http://www.edgeonline.com/

This is an online magazine for entrepreneurs. It contains a variety of features, including interviews with entrepreneurs, extensive training modules on many topics, and other resources of interest.

Entrepreneurs on the Web
http://www.eotw.com//EOTW.html

EOTW is a set of links to business-related resources. Included are resources related to Magazines & Journals, Government/Law, Financial, Services/Opportunities, Regional, and Entrepreneurial Organizations.

IdeasDigest
http://www.ideas.wis.net/

IdeasDigest is an online magazine devoted to innovation. In addition to products and services, the magazine offers articles, an events calendar, and other features for inventors and innovators.

Investor WEB
http://investorweb.com/

Investor WEB is an investment resource page which has several items of particular use for the entrepreneur. Included is a daily updated list of IPO's, a beginning investor's page, and links to other investment-oriented sites.

SCOR-net   http://www.scor-net.com/

This is the home page of the Small Corporate Offer Registration Network. It contains a listing of companies who have gone or are about to go public. It also contains links to resources useful to small companies seeking capital.

CEO-Access   http://www.ceo-access.com/index.html

CEO-Access is a "general information" business page, but focusses on links and resources of particular interest to the business owner. Many of the business links are entrepreneurial in nature.

Foundation   http://www.fed.org/fed/
for Enterprise
Development

FEDnet is devoted to helping companies learn about equity sharing (stock options, stock bonuses, 401(k) plans, ESOPS, etc.). Services and informational resources are available free.

Entrepreneurs   http://www.astranet.com/eexchange/
Exchange   jc00indx.htm

The Entrepreneurs Exchange is sponsored by Prodigy and features articles on any aspect of small business management. All articles are experiential in nature, written by small business owners, about their experiences and expertise.

Capital Quest	http://www.usbusiness.com/ capquest/home.html

Capital Quest is a forum for entrepreneurs to showcase their ideas and expose them to potential investors.   Fees are charged to feature an idea or concept.

Cyberpreneurs Guide to the Internet	gopher://una.hh.lib.umich.edu/00/ inetdirsstacks/cyberpren%3aschwilk

This gopher site provides a listing and descriptions of Internet resources related to entrepreneurial endeavors on the Internet.

International Business

The Global Business Forum	http://www.pragmatix.com/gbf/gbf.html

The Global Business Forum is a commercial endeavor providing online services related to importing/exporting.

Foreign Currency Exchange Rates	gopher://una.hh.lib.umich.edu:70/00/ ebb/monetary/tenfx.frb

This site provides current spot exchange rates (as of 10am daily), from the Federal Reserve Bank of New York.

International Business Resources on the WWW	http://ciber.bus.msu.edu/busres.htm

This site is a "links" page to numerous international business resources. It contains extensive lists of links on a variety of topics, including regional and country specific information, statistical data, company information, directories, government resources, trade shows, and other business WWW pages.

Currency Converter	http://www.olsen.ch/cgi-bin/exmenu

The Currency Converter provides the exchange rate (daily high, low, and median) for any day since January 1, 1990, for virtually any currency denomination.

Nijenrode's Foreign Stats and Economic Trends	gopher://zeus.nijenrode.nl/11/Business/ Statistics

This gopher site offers foreign statistics and economic trends for the world, by continent, and by country.

International Business Resources on the WWW	http://gnn.com/wic/wics/bus.47.html

International Business Resources provides links to a number of international trade-related resources, including regional, country specific, and governmental sources, and periodicals. It is maintained by Michigan State University's Center for International Business Education and Research.

The Global Trade Center

http://www.tradezone.com/tz/

The Global Trade Center is an extensive collection of links on global trade, global shopping, information on home-based global mail order selling, international business opportunities, and classified adds.

Citynet

http://www.city.net/

Citynet provides extensive information on regions, countries, and cities throughout the world through interactive maps, etc. For each destination, information regarding the culture, education, transportation, and much more is provided.

Small Business Management

U.S. Small Business Administration

http://www.sbaonline.sba.gov/

This is a link to this US Government agency. The SBA provides a number of useful resources related to starting, financing, and expanding small businesses as well as shareware to help run a small business, information on disaster aid, and other business-related information.

The Small Business Resource Center

http://www.webcom.com/seaquest/
sbrc/reports.html

This site offers an extensive collection of free reports for downloading. The reports cover a wide variety of topics of interest to the small business owner/manager. Topics range from developing a business plan to raising money, franchising, to information on a variety of specific home businesses like daycare, locksmithing, catering, secretarial, and many more.

Business Resource Center

http://www.kciLink.com/brc/

This site is provided by KCI Consulting, and offers several useful resources for small businesses. Advice-giving resources related to marketing, management, and financing are available, as are links to other useful sites.

SmallBizNet

http://www.lowe.org/smbiznet/index.htm

This site offers information services to small businesses and entrepreneurs. SmallBizNet Pointers contains an excellent collection of small business and entrepreneurship organized by business category (accounting, advertising, business plans, case studies, etc.). Sites are a mixture of very practical, manager-oriented and sites of interest to academics.

Preparing a Cash Flow Forecast

http://www.sb.gov.bc.ca/smallbus/
workshop/market/cashflow/cashflow.html

This British Columbia site provides a comprehensive, step-by-step guide to preparing a cash flow forecast for a small business.

Xerox   http://www.xerox.com/soho/
Small Business   resources.html
Resource Center

This site is offered as a service from Xerox and offers links to a variety of sites (mostly commercial sites) useful to small businesses. Despite the fact that the links are primarily commercial sites, most offer useful information in addition to information about their products or services.

IdeaCafe   http://www.IdeaCafe.com/

IdeaCafe is devoted to anything and everything related to small business management. It offers many features, from news to special guest interviews, resources, advice, etc. It's a fun site with very interesting graphics and style.

Small and   http://www.ro.com/small_business/
Home-based   homebased.html
Business Links

This is a useful set of links to resources of interest to small and home-based business owners and managers. Included are resources related to starting and running a business, as well as an extensive list of links to home-based business opportunities.

ADA for   http://www.usa.net/ada_infonet/
Small
Businesses

This site, devoted to the Americans with Disabilities Act, is maintained by the Small Business ADA Information Answer Center. The site offers resources which include information documents, training materials, referrals, and technical assistance.

On-Line Small Business Workshop	http://www.sb.gov.bc.ca/smallbus/ workshop/

The On-Line Small Business workshop takes the potential entrepreneur/manager through a process, from an idea to its evaluation, to protection of the idea through patents or trademarks.

Strategic Management

Business Policy and Strategy	http://comsp.com.latrobe.edu.au/bps.html

This is the home page of the Business Policy and Strategy Division of the Academy of Management. It provides access to the BPSNet discussion list, the BPS newsletter, bibliobraphies, and other resources

Management Research at Harvard	http://www.hbs.harvard.edu:80/research/ summaries/gm.html

This site provides summaries of current research activities at Harvard University in the areas of strategy, entrepreneurship, international business, and ethics.

Council on Competitiveness	http://nii.nist.gov/coc.html

This is the home page of the U.S. Council on Competitiveness. It provides background information on the council (objectives, key issues, etc.), as well as funding, projects, and work in process.

BIZStrat Business Strategy	http://128.172.188.1/isydept/faculty/ paiken/bizstrat/INDEX.HTM

This is a prototype of a strategy textbook companion designed to enhance a strategic management course.

Foundation for Enterprise Development (FEDnet)	http://www.fed.org/fed/

A business network for employee ownership issues, including equity compensation, employee involvement, and other emerging business practices.

The Business Resource Library	http://www.fed.org/fed/library.html

FEDnet's resources for entrepreneurs. Included are: Case Studies and Company Profiles, Best Practices Profiles, Research and Reference Materials, Government Policy and Legislation, Employee Ownership Research, etc.

Mailing Lists

General Instructions:
Unless otherwise noted, to subscribe to any of these listserves, send an e-mail message to the addresses listed below. Do not include a subject line. In the body of the e-mail message type:

subscribe (listserve name) (yourfirstname) (yourlastname)

For example, if your name is "John Smith", and you want to subscribe to "ENTREP-L ", send an email to "listserv@ksuvm.ksu.edu", leave the subject line blank, and type the following in the body of the message:

subscribe ENTREP-L John Smith

A confirmation memo will be sent to your e-mail address. It will include instructions for sending messages to the list, how to unsubscribe from the list, and other important list-related information.

COM-PRIV
Commercialization of the Internet
To subscribe: COM-PRIV-REQUEST@PSI.COM

ENTREP-L
To subscribe: listserv@ksuvm.ksu.edu
For the membership of the Entrepreneurs Division of the Academy of Management.

IBJ-L
To subscribe: LISTSERV@PONIECKI.BERKELEY.EDU
The electronic text of the Internet Business Journal

Moonlight-1
Moonlighting/Home Biz Mailing List
To subscribe: listserv@netcom.com

BUSETH-L
Business Ethics Computer Network
To subscribe: LISTSERV@UBVM.CC.BUFFALO.EDU

BETS-L
Business Ethics Teaching Society network
To subscribe: LISTSERV@UICVM.UIC.EDU

FAMILYBIZ
Family Business Discussion List
To subscribe: listproc@pwa.acusd.edu

IABS-L
Social Issues in Management
To subscribe: LISTSERV@PSUVM.PSU.EDU

BPS-NET
Business Policy and Strategy network
To subscribe: Contact Jim Stephenson at
STEPHENSON@XMAN.WHARTON.UPENN.EDU

Newsgroups

misc.entrepreneurs
misc.entrepreneurs.moderated
alt.business.misc
alt.business.import-export
misc.invest

Appendix

Other Business Links

This Appendix provides starting points for resources not related directly to management, including links to marketing, financial, and accounting resources. The references provided here can be described as very broad-based business-oriented indexes which will significantly enhance the searcher's ability to find specific resources related to virtually any aspect of business. These topics have been broken down into the following categories:

General Business
Business News
Business Humor

General Business Sites

IOMA   http://ioma.com:80/ioma/direct.html

This is the home page of the Institute of Management and Administration. It provides a list of business-related resources, organized alphabetically within several topic areas. Topics include several financial-related headings, human resources, insurance, etc.

Business Information Resources   http://www.eotw.com//business_info.html

This page offers six categories (Magazines and Journals, Government/Law, Financial, Services/Opportunities, Regional, and Entrepreneurial Organizations) of business-related resources.

General Business/ Management Internet Resources   http://www.cwru.edu/CWRU/UL/ MANAGEMENT/GeneralInternet.html

This site provides links to a variety of business resources organized by the following topics: Accounting, Banking and Finance, Economics, Labor and Human Relations, Management Information, Management Policy, Marketing, Operations Research, and Organizational Behavior.

BizLinks   http://www.execpc.com/~wmhogg/ bizlinks.html

BizLinks is a list of pointers to business schools, market reports, and general business resources.

A Business Researcher's Interests	http://www.pitt.edu/~malhotra/ interest.html

This site contains an extensive set of links to a broad range of business resources. Although a wide range of categories exist here, many are related to information management and technology.

Current Business Statistics Gopher	gopher://una.hh.lib.umich.edu/11/ebb/cbs

This University of Michigan site contains a collection of a wide range of business statistics through 1994. It contains the series published monthly by the Bureau of Economic Analysis.

LawTalk Business Law	http://www.law.indiana.edu/law/ bizlaw.html

This site contains audio files on a variety of legal topics.

Yahoo-- Business	http://www.yahoo.com/Business/

This is a direct link to Yahoo's "business and economy" section, searchable by keywords, or browsable through a list of business and economy subheadings.

FINWeb	http://finweb.bus.utexas.edu/finecon.html

This site provides a broad range of links to finance-related Internet resources. Included are links to journals, databases, and other financial pages.

All Business Network	http://www.all-biz.com/

The All Business Network provides a search function for business topics, access to articles and news, a reference desk with a variety of reference resources, etc.

Nerd World Media Business Index	http://www.nerdworld.com/users/ dstein/nw9.html

This site offers a topic-oriented index of business resources. Most links are business providers of services related to the topic.

Business Open Learning Archive	http://wwwbs.wlihe.ac.uk/~jarvis/ bola/

BOLA is a virtual course in a broad variety of business-oriented (mostly management) topics.

Net-squared Business	http://www.commerce.com/net2/ business/business.html

Net-squared is an extensive links page, organized by topic (accounting, finance, insurance, marketing, etc.). It provides extensive linkages to Internet sites relating to virtually any area of business.

Nijenrode Business Webserver	http://www.nijenrode.nl/resources/bus.html

The Nijenrode Business Webserver is designed to serve students, faculty, and researchers at business schools. It provides a search engine to search all of its resources and also has a hyperindex, organized by business topic.

Hoover's Online Corporate Directory	http://www.hoovers.com/

Hoover's is a directory of over 10,000 corporations, which can be searched by company name, state, city, size, etc., with links to the corporations' WWW sites.

SIC Codes	http://weber.u.washington.edu/~dev/sic.html

This University of Washington site provides a complete listing of the Standard Industrial Classification (SIC) Codes.

Research at the Harvard Business School	http://www.hbs.harvard.edu/research/contents.html

This is the main table of contents linking to current research activities at the Harvard Business School.

Business News

Newspage   http://www.newspage.com/

Newspage offers business news, by category, from over 600 information sources. Searches are possible within each category. Registration is required for full text, but it is free.

Yahoo's   http://www.yahoo.com/headlines/
Business   current/business/
Summary

This Yahoo site provides links to current business-related headlines.

Business Humor

Murphy's   http://dirac.bcm.tmc.edu:80/murphy.html
Law

This site contains Murphy's Law and many of its useful and humorous corollaries.

The Dilbert Zone	http://www.unitedmedia.com/comics/ dilbert/index.html

This site offers Dilbert's philosophical commentary on corporate life. Current and archived strips are available, daily and Sunday color, history, and everything you might want to know about Dilbert and his creator, Scott Adams.

Index

V

Veronica, 27
Virtual Tourist, 29

W

Webcrawler, 34
Whole Internet Catalog Select, 29
World Access Internet Navigator, 35
World Wide Web, 14
          searching, 27
WWW Worm, 34

Y

Yahoo, 29, 35